The Grid

BY THE SAME AUTHORS

This Book Is from the Future
A Journey through Portals, Relativity,
Wormholes, and Other Adventures in Time Travel

The Trinity Secret
The Power of Three and the Code of Creation

The Déjà Vu Enigma
A Journey through the Anomalies of Mind, Memory, and Time

The Resonance Key
Exploring the Links between Vibration,
Consciousness, and the Zero Point Grid

11:11—The Time Prompt Phenomenon
The Meaning behind Mysterious Signs,
Sequences, and Synchronicities

MARIE D. JONES
LARRY FLAXMAN

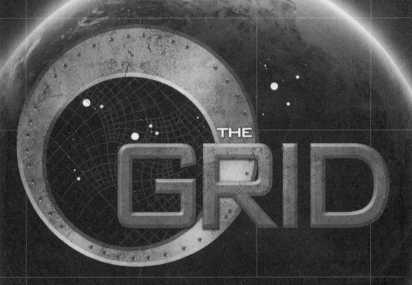

Hier⊕phantpublishing

Cover design by Adrian Morgan
Cover art © istockphoto.com
Author photo by Linda Belford Woods
Text design by Jane Hagaman

Hierophant Publishing
8301 Broadway, Suite 219
San Antonio, TX 78209
888-800-4240
www.hierophantpublishing.com

If you are unable to order this book from your local
bookseller, you may order directly from the publisher.

Library of Congress Control Number: 2013946634

ISBN 978-1-938289-21-7

10 9 8 7 6 5 4 3 2 1

Printed on acid-free paper in the United States

DEDICATION

To Mary Essa and Max

*And to Sheila and Norman Flaxman and John Savino,
who are out there, somewhere, walking the Grid.*

I am seeking for the bridge which leans from the visible to the invisible through reality.

—MAX BECKMANN

CONTENTS

PART THREE: WALKING THE GRID

PREFACE

An idea is meaningless without the inner conviction that it has the potential for being more than just an idea. When we authors joined forces back in 2007, after building careers and reputations on our own as solid researchers with a keen eye for the cutting edge, it was because of a simple Internet exchange. Our friendship, and our research, began in earnest over a growing body of shared ideals and common rationales that led to five books, dozens of articles, e-books, and research papers, not to mention hundreds of radio shows and events.

In truth, we were both just dreamers with a lust for thinking outside the box and pushing the envelope in our quest to understand the world around us. Making complex scientific concepts accessible for a lay audience brought us great success, and despite living over a thousand miles apart, here we are six years later, passionately involved in this concept we call the Grid.

The Grid grew from impassioned phone conversations—some late at night, others while sitting in parking lots talking for hours at a time—and thousands of emails that became a dance of ideas building up and breaking down and building up again as we grew ever closer to the breathless conclusion that, lo and behold, maybe we were on to something really big. A concept so profound that it could undoubtedly be considered a game changer.

The Grid

INTRODUCTION

If the doors of perception were cleansed, everything would appear as it is—infinite.
—WILLIAM BLAKE, "THE MARRIAGE OF HEAVEN AND HELL"

Reality . . . has a sliding door.
—RALPH WALDO EMERSON

What is reality?

Countless sages, scientists, philosophers, and spiritual leaders have asked that very question. Yet, even after centuries of inquiring, we still know little, if anything at all, about the true nature of reality. But perhaps there have been clues available to this great mystery all along, right in front of us, hidden in plain sight. Clues that suggest an actual structure, or more likely, an infrastructure, that is mirrored in the laws of science, spoken of in the holiest of religious texts, and is even evident in the construct of our own bodies, brains, and minds. A structure that we exist within, are a part of, and can even move about in. A structure that, once envisioned, opens us up to amazing new potentialities, abilities, and experiences we never imagined possible. A structure that science, spirituality, and metaphysics alike recognize. From the world of quantum physics and the zero-point field, the various levels of consciousness and altered states of mind, and the layered worlds of shamans and medicine healers, the concept of the Grid is found everywhere and goes by many names and variations.

A little more than five years ago, we came together from across the country with a shared interest and passion for finding answers to the biggest questions of human existence. Who are we? How did we get here? Do we have a purpose? Are there other worlds besides this one? We combined forces and partnered in a venture called ParaExplorers—a "pair of explorers." And explore we have, journeying into the unknown territories of worlds seen and unseen.

In our books we introduced a concept we refer to as "the Grid," an infrastructure of reality as a grid-like edifice, with contacts and connecting points that allow for traveling between levels (or layers) of reality. Imagine a skyscraper with multiple floors, and elevators and stairways leading from floor to floor. These various "connectors" represent the mechanisms by which we may be experiencing the Grid, and with practice we may be able to strengthen our ability to walk the Grid at will and access parallel universes, alternate dimensions, and worlds beyond the traditional confines of space and time as we understand them.

The basic concept has proven so popular that we felt compelled to expand upon the Grid and develop a more advanced model that would more completely describe the infrastructure of reality. The Grid is both a force and a source of all energy, matter, and form. It contains the entire landscape of time, from past to future.

Quantum physicists refer to it as the zero-point field—a grand, ground state of all there is that is both creative and regenerative. In this field, everything is in a state of superposition until the act of observation collapses the wave function into a fixed object in a fixed position. But before that happens, the field is filled with nothing but pure potential, where everything and anything exists. Quantum theory also points to parallel universes, additional spatial and temporal dimensions, even wormholes and portals—mechanisms that lead us from one point in one universe to another point in another universe. If this doesn't make sense right now, don't worry—we'll get into the details of how science supports our theory of the Grid in the course of this book.

Not only does science play a huge role in conceptualizing and understanding the Grid, so do religion and spirituality. Every religious tradition believes in some form of field or source of everything that we can move about in to discover new worlds. From the seven layers of heaven to the three worlds of shamanism, what science tells us about the Grid and the infrastructure of reality is mirrored in the teachings of spiritual sages from the beginning of recorded history. The Egyptian-Greek Hermetica wisdom texts tell of man, God, and the cosmic, from which all things come and all things return. Christ himself said, "In my father's house are many mansions"—a possible reference to levels of reality or perhaps even parallel universes. Even mythology, creation stories, and cosmogenesis stories of the great Sumerians, Babylonians, and Egyptians tell of a primordial nothingness from which everything sprang forth into being, and of the many worlds within worlds that nothingness contained.

Now, the most current research in quantum physics is backing up this concept of something coming from nothing, and we know now that "empty space" is really teeming with virtual particles popping in and out of existence. Both noetic sciences and metaphysics also speak of another level of reality—hidden implicate order, a field of intention, and an invisible web of connectivity that underlies all of existence, the source for all there is, was, and ever will be. This hidden order or infrastructure is both creative and regenerative, and some even theorize that it may well be conscious and evolving!

The Grid is a comprehensive examination of how all these aspects come together into one profound concept to present what we see, know, and sense just beneath the surface (beyond the veil, the paranormal, the anomalous, and the mysterious). We have spent years individually and collectively researching aspects of the Grid—what it is, how it is accessed, and how we can learn to use it to expand our awareness and empower our lives. Our grand unified theory of the scientific, metaphysical, and paranormal will explore:

- ◎ What is the Grid? What might it look like?
- ◎ How do matter and energy operate within the Grid?
- ◎ Information, information theory, and the Grid: Is this the Matrix?
- ◎ Do parallel universes and alternate dimensions exist in the Grid?
- ◎ How does time operate in the Grid? Is time travel possible?
- ◎ What connects one level of the Grid to another?

- How does the human brain/mind/consciousness create reality from the information in the Grid?

- Do paranormal phenomena such as ghosts, UFOs, psi abilities, and cryptids come from other levels of the Grid? How do they get here?

- Where do we come from, and where do we go when we die? What do near-death experiences and out-of-body experiences tell us about the Grid?

- Is the Grid organic, alive, conscious—or is it just a massive computer program?

- What do religion and myth say about the Grid?

- What do quantum, theoretical, and speculative physics say about the Grid?

- How might our own physiology allow us access to the Grid?

- Do certain environmental effects trigger access to the Grid?

- What is our role in shaping our personal and collective reality from the Grid?

We present the hidden structure of the Grid in three parts . . .

Part 1: The Infrastructure of the Grid

In the first part, we describe what the Grid might look like were it visible to the human eye, using simple analogies that describe levels of realities connected to each other by various means. The Grid is invisible; and yet we can describe it based on how it affects our reality, much like how we conceive of the force of gravity. We do not see gravity, but we can see its influences and effects on the world around us.

Part 2: Connectors, Triggers, and Mechanisms of the Grid

In part 2, we'll cover connectors, triggers, and mechanisms of the Grid. Connectors are the various bridges between levels of reality that link one to the other and allow for potential cross talk between levels. One of the key connectors is resonance, which we believe is a powerful tool for not only accessing realities but creating them as well. Consciousness is another connector.

Triggers and mechanisms allow us access to the connectors in the Grid, and thus the levels of the Grid itself. They can be interior/physiological elements in the human body and brain or exterior influences in the environment.

The Grid presents an intriguing and exciting possibility: that reality actually does have a form, a structure, and a blueprint . . . with layer upon layer of interlocking and intersecting realities that allow glimpses and passages to other levels. As we worked to further develop and fine-tune our concept, we came across many potential mechanisms by which we may access and travel the Grid. Resonance (which we wrote a book about exclusively), vibration, and frequency all seem to play key roles in perceiving and experiencing alternate realities, just as in everyday reality. Resonance in particular is proving to be a potential means for raising and altering brain waves, transforming consciousness, and shifting perception, all with the use of sound and vibration. Science tells us that in the natural world, two objects that become in sync or align at the same vibratory rate find their own special resonance, which may allow for the creation of new matter, energy, and forms, as well as open new doors and windows to other dimensions.

Part 3: Walking the Grid

If reality is the Grid, and resonance the connector, then how do we summon the right frequency, the right vibration, that will allow us to move about and experience other levels of the Grid?

We believe that the key to traveling the Grid lies entirely in the power of intention. The thrilling science of noetics (made famous in Dan Brown's best-selling novel *The Lost Symbol*) teaches us that consciousness, intention, and thought are energetic, creative, and far more involved in the perception, and actual manifestation, of our personal and collective realities than we ever imagined.

Even the massive best seller *The Secret* suggests that we can manifest reality according to the vibration of our thoughts and intentions. Dr. Wayne Dyer, in his book *The Power of Intention,* talks of an "omnipresent intention" that is invisible and formless yet contains within it every thought, idea, concept, and eventual manifestation, and acts as the manager of it all.

Intention, like resonance, may be an actual mechanism by which we can use the energy and information present in the many layers of the Grid to create our reality! Physicist David Bohm wrote of this in his book *Wholeness and the Implicate Order,* positing that all ordering influence and information are present in the invisible domain of higher reality, and they can be called upon when needed. This means we are not only living in the Grid, but we are the Grid itself, determining through choice and free will which layer or destiny we will experience as real.

Carlos Castaneda wrote of intent as a "force that exists in the universe. When Sorcerers—those that live of the Source—

beckon intent, it comes to them and sets up the path for attainment." More than two thousand years ago, Patanjali suggested the same when he wrote of "dormant forces, faculties and talents" that we all have access to in order to become the best we can be. In the levels of the Grid, these dormant forces dance, waiting for us to notice them and make use of them.

From the quantum to the cosmic, the natural to the supernatural, and the scientific to the spiritual, the Grid offers a potentially profound explanation for everything that we know to be true—and everything we don't. The Grid theory can help to explain the existence of paranormal phenomena, life after death and past lives, time travel, parallel universes, alternate dimensions, extrasensory perception (ESP) and psi abilities, déjà vu, precognition, remote viewing, psychic abilities, ghosts, cryptids, UFOs, and other anomalies that up until now defied explanation. In fact, many experts in the fields of ufology, ghosts and spirits, and cryptozoology suggest that there may be strong evidence for an interdimensional explanation for these phenomena. For in the many levels of the Grid are worlds that we can only imagine, and some we probably are incapable of even envisioning. Yet, perhaps, we sometimes get a glimpse of them when we experience such things as precognitive dreams, a strong déjà vu event, or the ability to "know" information we have no access to.

But none of this really matters unless we can put the power of knowledge to work in our individual lives, and the Grid offers a potent self-help and personal empowerment aspect that parallels the teachings of ancient spiritual masters from Buddha to Christ, as well as the modern sages today who talk of the Secret of intention and reality. In knowing the Grid's "dormant forces," how it works, as well as how to work it, we can truly transform and enlighten people individually and (we hope) collectively. Learning to see beyond what our five senses tell us is real, and knowing that we always have access to all the information, wisdom, and guidance we need can transform a life—and a planet.

Come with us as we explore the many layers of reality that make up this vast and perhaps infinite infrastructure of parallel universes, alternate dimensions, multiple realities, and levels of awareness that boggle the mind and fire up the imagination. Join us as we examine the role of resonance, the body and mind and brain, and the power of consciousness to serve as the mechanisms, and the machine operators, that allow us access to the Grid just as an elevator allows us access to other floors in a tall skyscraper.

Come with us as we walk the Grid.

Part One

The Infrastructure of the Grid

CHAPTER 1

REALITY 101

What Is the Grid? Exploring the Invisible Infrastructure of Reality

Do we need more reality? We've already got so much.
—RALPH ABRAHAM, *THE EVOLUTIONARY MIND*

Man is the only animal for whom his own existence is a problem which he has to solve.
—ERICH FROMM, *MAN FOR HIMSELF*

Those who came before us, and others at this very time, are formulating their own theories about the nature of reality. History is rampant with great minds and brilliant thinkers seeking to understand the way the world works, the seen and the unseen. The science of reality itself. Religions and myth, spiritual and native traditions, New Age gurus and metaphysicians, scientists and philosophers, have all tossed their input into the hat from which we have molded and shaped our theory. We figured it was our turn to throw something into the hat ourselves.

Trying to describe the nature of reality is like trying to describe air. It is invisible. We cannot put in under a microscope, or hold it in our hands to show our friends, or make it perform on a YouTube video. Yet we live day-to-day with the effects of its presence. We know air exists because we would die if we didn't breathe it in and out of our lungs to nourish our brain and blood cells and tissues. We know it is there, yet in a court of law we could never put it on the witness stand.

Such is the case with trying to describe reality. We run into problems with verbiage. It's the All. It's existence. It's the matrix of being. It's what we experience each day and night. It's what we live in. Yet none of these definitions really quite captures the possible "structure" of reality in a way we can wrap our minds around. We know reality is there. At least the illusion of it is. Reality encompasses everything, including us, within its hidden grasp, and we experience the effects all around us as our five senses perceive and process our surroundings.

But were we to give a form to reality in its entirety what might it be like? Since no one has really been able to photograph it or offer up valid proof of its physical form, we must go on more circumstantial evidence. In fact, this is the case when trying to describe anything that is invisible or beyond the normal experience. We have to resort to two things:

1. Coming up with analogies and symbols that simplify the complexity of what we are trying to describe.
2. Presenting the surrounding evidence of its existence by showing how it influences the things around it.

In this chapter, we will focus on a simple symbolic analogy. In future chapters we will present the surrounding evidence of this theory, and hopefully by the time you are done reading this book you will look at reality in a whole new way. Our goal is that you will see reality itself as possibly having an actual form, one that has function and laws and operates in a very specific manner to create the entirety of human existence.

This is where the power of imagination comes into play. Were reality to have an actual infrastructure within which we live and move and have our being, what would we liken that structure to?

THE SHAPE OF REALITY

We know that we exist in a reality that we collectively share with everyone on the planet. In this singular reality a chair is a chair, and a dog is a dog, and though we might have different languages with different words to describe such things, the things themselves are the same for all of us. We know that we move around in a world with certain rules and laws of nature and physics, laws that govern how things operate both in the heavens and here on Earth . . . even in our own bodies. These laws and forces serve as the foundation from which life itself springs forth, and we can see the results as our manifest physical reality.

To this we add an individual reality, one we each carry with us from birth to death, shaded and molded by parental influence, social conditioning, cultural influence, environmental factors, education, and religious belief. Our individual reality is our own, even as it consists of many things we mutually agree upon with those around us. In a sense, the collective and the individual realities blend and have fluid boundaries for the most part. (In extreme cases, such as with native tribes living deep in the Amazon rainforest, reality may not be anything like what we perceive it as, simply because of differing influences and factors. Yet there is still a collective understanding of being human . . . and of existing within a framework that has physical laws and forces, even if the native explanation is far different from our modern scientific one.)

Reality is for the most part our totality of existence, perceivable through the five senses of taste, smell, sight, hearing, and touch, and the experiences we gather since birth to accumulate into a singular lifetime.

But . . . we sense, and often even directly experience, evidence of something else. Something unnamable and unknowable, a reality, or realities, just beyond the "veil" of the five senses. A reality, or realities, just beyond the boundaries of normal day-to-day life and the mundane experiences it contains. Now and then, we experience something that shakes us out of our comfort zone and shocks us into the realization that there is much more to reality than meets the eye.

Beyond the veil of the illusion of our one singular reality, there may even be an infinite number of other levels of existence, where things we cannot even imagine exist, things that sometimes cross into our reality in the form of unusual, paranormal, supernatural, or mysterious events. These forms can take on many shapes, such as dreams that predict a future event, psychic abilities, visions, healings, seeing a ghost or encountering a mysterious entity, entering a time slip or a shift in consciousness, or even traveling into the astral plane. These are just a few of the many ways that we might be moving between realities, voluntarily or accidentally.

The levels of reality are like a three-dimensional grid that consists of layers of realities stacked on top of and alongside one another, each connected to the others in an interlocking cube. This is the Grid.

Perhaps in this grid we speak of, there are finite levels and layers of realities. That would imply an end to entirety, which for some is an impossible thing to even imagine. Does the universe have an end? Are there other universes out there? How many? Ten? Twenty? Two million? Imagine each universe as a separate level of this grid. How would they end? Wouldn't there be something just beyond the "end" boundary?

Perhaps there is an infinite number of levels in the Grid, with no end and no beginning, even as there may be an end and a beginning to a single level. Imagine our own universe and the big bang. In chapter 2 on the science of the Grid, we look at how the big bang may have been the beginning "singularity point" for only one Grid level, but not all of them. Each level may have a big bang all its own, with bangs going on all the time, creating new levels of the Grid as others die off.

Or perhaps the Grid is like a snowball rolling downhill, building exponentially in size and capacity as it gathers more snow to its core. It may even be self-regenerating, so that when one level breaks down another rises out of the ashes and creates even more levels from its origin point.

We will explore all of these possibilities in later chapters, but for the sake of understanding the infrastructure itself, and how it might work, let's imagine our Grid as a finite and easily identifiable shape: a skyscraper.

Were we to look inside a skyscraper being erected, we would see levels sitting atop and aside one another, each with its own floor filled with rooms and windows and doorways—the skeleton, if you will. One floor alone might have a hundred different rooms in which different activities take place. These rooms are connected with doors and hallways, allowing the people on that particular floor the freedom to move about between rooms.

In a skyscraper there are many floors, each with its own world of possibilities. Perceptually, each floor is a reality in and of itself, a closed existence that is filled with experiences and events for those who live and work on that particular floor. Those who wish to experience the reality of another floor may easily do so by simply taking the elevator, the stairs, or perhaps the exterior fire escape, for there are many connectors in this Grid of reality allowing movement and interaction.

Imagine the Grid as having various access points. Accessing the top floor takes more energy and effort than accessing the floors immediately above or below your own reality. Beyond the energy requirements, we may also be programmed to believe that our own reality is hard enough to deal with without complicating it by constantly moving between levels. And yet, that opportunity is present in this Grid.

Now zoom out a bit further. Imagine your skyscraper as part of a complex of several buildings, each representing a "bundle" of parallel worlds or realities. This mirrors the concepts of the most cutting-edge quantum and speculative physics, which will be examined in later chapters.

Figure 1. A skyscraper under construction provides a perfect visual for how the Grid infrastructure might appear. *Courtesy of FlickerView/Wikimedia Commons*

Another concept to be explored is that of bubble universes. Bubble universes may contain wormholes and portals connecting to other bubble universes, similar to the way one section of a building leads to another section.

The Grid, then, acts as an infrastructure of realities layered upon and alongside each other, with access points that allow travel and interaction between layers. These access points act as the elevators and staircases between worlds, and as we will discover, they can occur spontaneously or purposefully depending on a variety of factors, including human physiology, psychology, environmental influences, and even anomalies that all align to allow for an

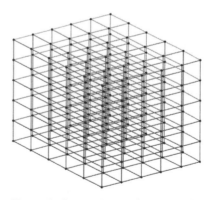

Figure 2. Our point in the Grid of realities is like a dot on a line grid. *Courtesy of Tex.Stackexchange*

opening to present itself between the layers or levels of the Grid of existence. If we know what the connectors are and where they are located, we can walk this Grid, and thus experience the many floors that we call the entirety of existence.

You Are Here

We exist at one finite point in the Grid, and yet our influence can be felt throughout the levels, as a pebble thrown into a still pond creates a ripple effect that moves outward until its influence is too weak to have an effect. We, too, may have this ripple effect on the layers of the Grid that we are closest to or are able to access. What we do in our level of the Grid may no doubt affect what happens in other levels, unless certain protectors and barriers are in place to prevent such influence.

Like time travel, there may be paradoxes or natural and physical barriers in place that keep us from entering parts of the Grid where we don't belong or that we are not equipped to handle. Perhaps our level of consciousness even dictates where and when we can move about the Grid, much like an employee in an office must have permission to leave his or her floor to go to another floor for lunch, a break, or interaction with another department in the company.

In future chapters we will go further in depth into all of the aspects of the Grid, from the connectors and mechanisms by which we move about the Grid, to the aspects of our own bodies, brains, and consciousness that may dictate the ability to walk the Grid, to what other levels may look like and what kinds of laws might govern them, as well as what kinds of "things" might reside there. These other realities may be much like ours in many cases, and unimaginably different as well.

Some may transcend time and space as we understand them, curving and warping into different universes with their own grid-like realities, yet all a part of the ultimate skyscraper that we call the Grid. Like a city skyline with many buildings reaching to the sky, the Grid itself then becomes the skyline, with people moving between buildings, and between worlds, by foot or boat or car or trolley or bicycle. No matter the analogy, this Grid is an interlocking infrastructure that may be of infinite size and complexity, containing all that was, is, and ever will be.

It is, simply, All. The whole darn city itself.

Zoom out once again, and imagine that each skyscraper in a major city skyline is a universe unto itself. In one universe, one level of reality, there may be the hustle and bustle of energy and activity, and yet a nearby building may be under construction and void of activity. And if the actual Grid contains infinite skylines, one entire city may be a ghost town long dead to life and energetic exchange, and another city may be waiting to be born from the blueprints of a Master Architect's imagination.

Even within just one reality, just one skyscraper, those same contrasts may exist, with one floor loud and bustling, with people moving and interacting and doing their thing, and the floor right above it abandoned, silent, still. As above, so below, and the individual "reality" we call home may actually be a mirror of the greater cosmic reality that contains the entirety of the Grid. This is a powerful concept in most spiritual traditions, the idea that each level of the Grid may, as a holographic image, contain the greater whole of the entire

Grid itself. And perhaps our brains behave in this same holographic manner, mirroring the Grid on a physiological and neurological scale that creates our perception, belief, conditioning, and ultimately the actual experience of physical reality that we engage in from the moment of birth to the moment of death. Although, in the Grid birth and death are merely elevator rides that begin and end on particular floors, and they say nothing of the floors that came before or those that come after we take our last breath.

LOOPS AND PERCEPTIONS

Reality is about perception, and much of what we call reality is nothing more than the accumulation of experience, memory, expectation, and habit. We experience the same things over and over again and react and respond in similar fashion more often than not to create a loop of experience that we call life. Yet, reality has never been accepted at face value by the world's religions, native belief systems, metaphysicians, philosophers, sages, or scientists. All have known of these other potentialities, these other realities in the Grid, even if they could not offer tangible, empirical proof of them, other than the subjective experiences of millions, perhaps billions of people who at some point in their "normal" lives walk the other floors or levels of the Grid.

We present an infrastructure of the All of reality that offers a visual of levels and connectors, spreading outward from some center point, yet having no center, really, because in this Grid there is all of eternity. The center may be where we are; yet we exist fully within this Grid. We live and move and have our being in it. And we can move to any other floor or room or office or building we want depending on the factors and circumstances our theory of the Grid sets forth.

"In my father's house are many mansions . . ." Many mansions . . . many levels. Many doors and windows and staircases and connectors. Perhaps you've even walked one of these levels yourself already . . .

CHAPTER 2

MULTIPLE WORLDS

Levels of the Grid

Reality is not what it is. It consists of the many realities which it can be made into.

—WALLACE STEVENS, *OPUS POSTHUMOUS*

The word universe is supposed to mean everything that exists. Today, we're almost certain that our universe is not all there is. There really could be parallel earths, parallel yous, and parallel mes. It's hard not to wonder what our alter egos might be like, whether they're living out our most cherished dreams. But, don't forget this possibility: You could already be living the dream of another you from a parallel universe.

—MORGAN FREEMAN, *CURIOSITY: IS THERE A PARALLEL UNIVERSE?*

Go then. There are other worlds than these.

—STEPHEN KING, *THE GUNSLINGER*

Levels. Worlds. Universes. Are these simply the ideas of science fiction and fantasy, or is there an actual science behind a grid-like structure of reality? Descriptions of multiple and parallel worlds, alternate dimensions of space and time, and realities that lie hidden beneath the visible order of our own abound in theoretical and quantum physics. Tracking the science of the Grid is like going on a long scavenger hunt of clues and links in knowledge and revelation that comes to one stunning conclusion: There are other worlds besides our own.

String Theory

One of the current pet theories of physics involves invisible strings, open and closed and straight and looped, that oscillate at different vibratory frequencies. According to string theory, this would help to explain form and matter. Initially, string theory was proposed as a means of uniting quantum mechanics and general relativity to create a ToE, or theory of everything, that would adequately and mathematically describe, well, everything. The theory posits that elementary particles such as electrons and quarks within the atom are not zero-dimensional objects, but are instead open and closed one-dimensional oscillating strings, and that these strings carry an actual gravitational force.

Strings could have a number of different resonances, or patterns of vibration, that can correspond to various mass and elementary particle charges as well as create them. Strings with a greater amplitude and wavelength would correspond to a particle with greater energy and mass, while those with a lower amplitude and wavelength correspond to particles with less energy and mass. These variations of frequency and vibration would be the basic building blocks of all we see and perceive as form and matter and energy.

One way to look at this kind of oscillation or resonance is to think of a guitar string. Imagine how when the string is plucked along a different place on the neck of a guitar it will produce a different sound or note. Groupings of notes create different chords. Now, when applied to string theory, the groupings of various oscillating strings produce different energy and matter and form in a particulate sense.

String theory has its roots in Einstein's general relativity and classical unification (although the actual theory itself eluded Einstein until his death) and was later developed in the late 1960s as a theory involving subatomic hadrons (particles that feel the strong nuclear force interaction). Supported by such noted brilliant physicists as Stephen Hawking, Leonard Susskind, and Edward Witten, the theory has also been expanded over time into several superstring theories that suggest there are objects with numerous dimensions (anywhere from zero to nine) that incorporate multiple dimensions of time. These "branes," or membranes, may contain actual universes, and the collision of such branes may be what led to our own big bang . . . and the big bangs of other universes being born parallel to ours.

Our recognizable universe might be a "3-brane" floating in a higher dimension of space, according to Lisa Randall, Harvard physicist and author of *Warped Passages: Unraveling the Mysteries of the Universe's Hidden Dimensions*. Randall examines the brane theory as well as alternate dimensions of space and time—an integral part of the mathematics behind deconstructing the cosmos into its most basic components. In fact, our universe may be just a little fishy swimming in a virtual sea of other membranes, all encompassed within a super massive universe that we can only imagine the scale of.

In 1995, Edward Witten, one of the proponents of the existence of M-Theory, or "mother theory," stated that the *M* could stand for "magic, mystery, or membrane, depending on your taste." What is so magical is the concept that M-branes could contain hidden universes that exist alongside our own. The search for the most fundamental level of reality, whether it's the particles that make up physical objects, or the actual source field from which they spring, is the Holy Grail of physics and the object of pursuit of most scientists, metaphysicians, and spiritual teachers alike.

So, where does it all start? Is there a bottom level, a "ground floor" to the Grid? If so, that would imply that the grid-like shape of all there is has a finite quality, and that it ends somewhere. But what is beyond the end? Could there really be other dimensions beyond our own three spatial and one temporal ones, existing at the tip of our noses?

The inclusion of other dimensions, often even a suggestion of infinite dimensions, is a mainstay of theoretical physics when discussing string theory and other related theories. In order for these theories to "work" or be mathematically sound, these extra dimensions are necessary. They could be so tiny, though, as to be imperceptible, and exist entirely on a quantum scale. Or, they could be so huge and infinite as to be beyond our comprehension. No matter what, they are not just the fodder of fantasy and science fiction stories anymore.

BEYOND THREE DIMENSIONS

From a young age, we are taught that our world consists of height, width, and depth—a wholly three-dimensional reality. Add the dimension of time, and we now have a four-dimensional reality. But imagine eleven or twenty-two or thirty or even an infinite number of other dimensions of space alone, and it boggles the mind. Evolution has demanded our brains perceive only a three-dimensional world around us, but perhaps one day there will be a need for the brain to open up to the perception of other dimensions that for now are barely even imaginable on a computer.

A cube is a perfect example of the three spatial dimensions to which our existence is confined. Many attempts have been made to try to describe a four-dimensional hypercube, a cube within a cube. A six-dimensional object known as the Calabi-Yau manifold (named after Eugenio Calabi and Shing-Tung Yau) is an important concept in superstring theory. And Theodor Kaluza and Oskar Klein's Kaluza-Klein theory tried to bridge the forces of gravitation and electromagnetism by suggesting there was a fifth dimension so compact it was actually imperceptible.

It could, however, only be a matter of tweaking our brains to perceive a new dimension, and once done, we would never be able to "unperceive it." Now imagine another dimension of time, too! Could that even be possible? According to Sir Martin Reese, Astronomer Royal of the United Kingdom, if we were to find a new dimension of time we would literally have to create new words to describe more tenses than past, present, and future!

While these extra dimensions are mathematically probable, they are still very much theoretical. Yet they speak of other "realities" in the Grid that go beyond the confines of measurement and positioning of our own. What more could there be than height, depth, and width? Past, present, and future? Maybe one day we will find out.

Parallel Universes

From M-Theory we jump to parallel universes, which expands upon the idea that we are not only not alone in a planetary sense, but in a cosmic sense as well. For just as there are millions, if not billions, of other planets, there may also be millions of other universes. The notion of other universes has been a mainstay of science fiction and fantasy for hundreds of years—from the world beyond the magical wardrobe of C. S. Lewis's fantasy series the Chronicles of Narnia, and the portal-like rabbit hole of Lewis Carroll's *Alice's Adventures in Wonderland,* to the too-numerous-to-mention science fiction movies, novels, and television series that utilize the concept. But do hard science and physics buy into this idea of levels of existence, invisible yet parallel to us, and teeming with a reality all their own?

Theoretical physics adores parallel universes, even if there is no proof yet that they do exist. In his book *The Hidden Reality: Parallel Universes and the Deep Laws of the Cosmos,* popular physicist Brian Greene looks back to childhood memories of opening a closet door with a mirror upon it and seeing that when the mirror aligned with another mirror on his wall it created a "seemingly endless series of reflections of anything situated between them." This fascinating image led him to think about his many reflected selves entering "an imaginary parallel world" made of both light and imagination.

Greene admits that the original definition of the word *universe* meant everything . . . all there is. But over time, new ideas and theories have led to a redefinition to capture a much larger, wider canvas of parallel, multiple, and alternate universes that are all part of an infinite whole. . . . Universe then actually becomes megaverse, metaverse, multiverse. We are truly not alone.

Greene also writes of the varied qualities of these many worlds: "In some, the parallel universes are separated from us by enormous stretches of space or time; in others, they're hovering millimeters away; in others still, the very notion of their location proves parochial, devoid of meaning." Not only that, but when it comes to the actual laws that govern these universes, again we are met with such diversity. In some, the physical laws will be the same as ours, and in others the laws might be so different we wouldn't even perceive them or understand them. They might appear as magic to us.

Theoretical physicist Michio Kaku has written extensively about parallel universes and categorized them according to three distinct types:

- Hyperspace
- The multiverse
- Quantum parallel universes

In his books *Physics of the Impossible: A Scientific Exploration into the World of Phasers, Force Fields, Teleportation and Time Travel* and *Parallel Worlds: A Journey through*

Creation, Higher Dimensions, and the Future of the Cosmos, Kaku dives into the deep physics of such possible worlds, from string theory to what happened before the big bang to the concept of bubble universes connected by wormholes (more on those in chapter 4). Of his three categorizations, different measures of reality emerge.

HYPERSPACE

Is there a fourth spatial dimension? We know that we are trapped in a three-dimensional world of height, width, and length and that all possible positions can be described with these three coordinates. Hyperspace suggests that perhaps there is a fourth spatial dimension (we now call time the fourth dimension, but it is a temporal one!), something once deemed utterly impossible. Actually, this would be considered the fifth dimension, including that of time. But seriously . . . a fourth *spatial* dimension? Thanks to physicist Theodor Kaluza, who in 1919 hinted in a controversial scientific paper of higher dimensions, we may one day perceive what our brains, as of now, refuse to perceive. Kaluza proposed that if light is a wave, what is waving? If light, then, passes through the vacuum of space, what is waving in the vacuum? Thus the proposal that light is waves/ripples in the fifth dimension.

The term hyperspace describes something positioned in a higher dimension. Various string theories require ten or more dimensions to be mathematically sound, so a fourth dimension should be a piece of cake. But try visualizing it. It's impossible (or is it?) for our brains to grasp a new spatial dimension. In the fourth dimension, someone might be floating just above us, invisible, as written about by the famed H. G. Wells in *The*

Invisible Man. When we hear that string theory may require eleven dimensions, our brains virtually shut down, unable to even comprehend what any of them might look like, let alone what laws may govern them.

Bubble Universes

Hyperspatial dimensions give way to the theory of bubble universes, which are connected to one another via a wormhole-type mechanism. The bubble universes can rub against each other, bang together, and split apart and then suddenly just "pop" and no longer exist. Perhaps these bubble universes even float on the membranes of M-Theory, each its own reality yet part of a higher dimensional space. Perhaps they even have their own temporal reality as well, meaning that each universe operates on its own timeline, opening the door to time travel beyond the pesky paradoxes that insist we cannot change the past without altering the present and future.

Cosmologist Stephen Hawking calls these bubbles "baby universes" and believes that they connect through a system of tiny wormholes too small for humans to ever travel through. We would not be able to communicate with other bubble or baby universes, confined to our own corner of three-dimensional reality in the Grid. In a sense, we are stuck to our own membrane and cannot unstick ourselves to jump onto another world (unless we find the mechanism by which to do so!). Gravity, however, can move between these dimensions.

THE MULTIVERSE

There can be an infinite number of infinitesimally tiny or massively huge universes out there. Perhaps some are teeming with life; others are dead as doornails; and others are in between at all stages of evolution and growth. Because the laws of nature operating in each universe may be so vastly different, any forms of life that exist on these other levels of reality might be different too. In fact, life as we know it may not exist at all in many of these universes, with entities and forms so bizarre that we cannot even begin to envision them. These worlds may contain types of matter that look nothing like what we know of in our cosmic neck of the woods. In fact, atoms themselves might consist of stable matter we don't know about, unlike our own atoms made of protons, electrons, and neutrons.

Yet on other worlds, life may be pretty much similar to what it's like here on Earth, because no doubt there will be a number of other Earth-like planets orbiting a sun at just the right speed and distance to allow for the biological and chemical processes of life, even DNA, to emerge just as they did here.

The multiverse theory basically states that there are multiple universes that account for all that ever was, is, and will be and make up the entirety of creation—the Grid itself. The term multiverse was coined by an American psychologist, William James, in 1895, and it is sometimes mixed up with parallel universes and alternate dimensions. It is interesting that a psychologist would coin such a term, but the multiverse has become a popular concept in regards to a variety of arenas of study, including physics, cosmology, transpersonal psychology, philosophy, logic, and even metaphysics and the paranormal.

According to cosmologist Max Tegmark, one of the fathers of the parallel universe theory, it can be categorized into four levels. Tegmark proposes that Level I universes exist beyond our cosmological horizon and may contain physical constants and laws just like our own; Level II universes have different physical constants; and Level III universes encompass the many-worlds interpretation (MWI), a quantum theory of the multiverse. This MWI is the most fascinating of all concepts when it comes to potential levels of the Grid, and how they might form. Level IV universes are called the "ultimate ensemble" and consider as real all universes that are described by different mathematical structures and are the highest of the hierarchy of the multiverse.

QUANTUM PARALLEL UNIVERSES

Physicist Hugh Everett III introduced the many-worlds interpretation of quantum universes in 1957. His theory was part of a dissertation positing that reality might actually be made up of many worlds that arise each time a quantum event occurs, splitting off like branches growing on a tree. Imagine a new universe popping up every time a different choice is made at the quantum level, with an infinite and continuing number of universes springing forth in a mind-boggling array of potential realities.

In *Physics of the Impossible,* Michio Kaku suggests that the universe may exist in many parallel states defined by the wave function of the universe itself. The wave function refers to the ability of light to behave as both particle and wave until the act of observation or measurement "collapses the wave function" and gives fixed position to the particle(s). In this manner, the universe has many various states of potentiality and only when one reality is collapsed from the wave function into a fixed state do we get a physical manifestation of that reality. This universal wave function contains within it every possible configuration of a quantum object, thus allowing for everything that can be possible to become so.

So imagine a wave of possibilities, and each time an observer collapses that wave and fixes a possibility into position, a new universe breaks off from the original wave. This happens again and again and again to accommodate all other possible outcomes. In a sense, all possible positions and potentialities exist before they are observed into fixed form. Everything is real in a state of superposition, but not in a physical sense. Physicist David Deutsch called them "shadow universes," suggesting that many of the universes would be similar, if not identical, to our own, with possibly over a *trillion* potential universes!

Once again, could we experience or contact these other worlds, realities, states, or levels of the Grid physically? Kaku believes that it certainly cannot be ruled out, but it is highly unlikely—at least at the quantum level. However, in a cosmic sense, where again these universes may be like bubbles floating around in a big cosmic "bubble bath," it might be possible. And if we were able to somehow establish contact, perhaps they might be home to advanced civilizations. These civilizations might even be far more evolved and progressive than our own, and may have even harnessed the power of huge atom smashers, accomplished time travel, or figured out a host of other futuristic benchmarks that we now only consider the fodder of science fiction.

Zero-Point Field

We now understand that there is no such thing as empty space. There is no vacuum, no nothingness out there. Instead, there is a fundamental source field of energy at the quantum level, where subatomic particles pop in and out of existence in a foaming sea of virtual realities, like the spray off a thunderous waterfall or ocean wave.

The zero-point field (ZPF) is considered by many to be the true vacuum state of existence, but where fluctuations in the field are detectable at the lowest energy state, or the temperature of absolute zero. This field teems with zero-point energy that is the closest yet to zero we have gotten in the subatomic state.

In her book *The Field: The Quest for the Secret Force of the Universe,* award-winning investigative journalist Lynne McTaggart documents the discovery and potential of the zero-point field, describing it as "a repository of all fields and all ground energy states and all virtual particles—a field of fields. Every exchange of every virtual particle radiates energy." All of these virtual particles make up the vast and inexhaustible energy source that forms the background of empty space. Put simply, it is the most fundamental, rock-bottom level of "reality" there is. Some in the metaphysical world have described the ZPF as the "field of pure potentiality," or the "field of all possibility," where everything and anything that has or will ever exist does so in a virtual state waiting to be made manifest.

This field is also self-regenerating, as discovered by physicist Hal Puthoff, who has extensively researched and worked with ZPF and the extraction of energy from the field. According to Puthoff's research, the field acts as a "self-regenerating feedback loop across the cosmos," with fluctuations in the field waves driving the motion of subatomic particles. The motion of the particles in the universe in turn generate the ZPF, like a cat chasing its own tail. The field, then, can never be empty or run out of energy, for it is always feeding back into itself and creating new source energy that makes up all we know of as reality, both seen and unseen and yet to be seen.

This fundamental state of reality would also be an encoder and carrier of information that is imprinted upon the field. Hal Puthoff states, "If all subatomic matter in the world is interacting constantly with this ambient ground-state energy field, the subatomic waves of the field are constantly imprinting a record of the shape of everything . . . In a sense, the vacuum is the beginning and the end of everything in the universe." Information includes everything that was, is, and ever will be in our universe, and possibly others, and this information is in itself a fundamental aspect of reality. We may be nothing more than an information imprint; born of the field; and one day we will go back to the field.

This is the base of the Grid.

There are possibly an infinite number of these levels in the Grid, connected to each other through various means. Each level can exist entirely on its own, with little if any contact with other levels, unless of course the right triggers and mechanisms are discovered to activate the connectors. Some of the levels may be "dead" or dying, and others filled with life beyond our wildest imaginings. Some may be invisible or have such bizarre physical properties, attributes, and laws that we would have no physical (or even psychological) means of perceiving or processing them.

Some might be just like our own level. (Déjà vu, anyone?)

In terms of a hierarchy of levels of reality, the most fundamental level would be likened to the zero-point field, where nothingness becomes somethingness, and virtual reality becomes fixed reality. This would equate with the basement or lowest parking level of our skyscraper. From this level, we might suggest that there is a sense of progression or evolution of universes or realities, depending on how long they've existed and how many factors that correspond to the emergence of life are available.

Life as we know it arose because of very specific mathematical ratios of chemicals, gasses, and elements present after the big bang, leading to a perfect scenario, or a "Goldilocks zone," as physicist Paul Davies refers to it. Also known as the anthropic principle, this is where everything is not too hot, not too cold, but just right for life to crawl forth from the biochemical soup and evolve to higher forms. Should any of these ratios be tweaked plus or minus even the most minute of measurements, we would not be here. Or maybe we would, but we may have evolved into quite different life-forms.

Our level of the Grid appears to be finely tuned for life, but other levels may not be so accommodating. According to the cosmologist and astrophysicist Sir Martin Rees, this fine-tuning may be evidence that the multiverse does indeed exist, and that the physical constants that allow for life may or may not be present in a large number of these parallel realities. In other words, we got plumb lucky!

The zero-point energy of the field, the fluctuating virtual quantum state, and superstrings vibrating at various resonances—these are the most basic building blocks of energy that give way to all form and matter at the bottom level of the Grid. From these vibrations come solid, fixed, formed reality, depending on perhaps the observer or some predetermined blueprint that is embedded in the grand, ground state.

The "creative" level of the Grid, then, may be an energetic blueprint with infinite possibilities as to the kinds of structures that can be built upon its foundations. Each level from this point on is like a wall or door or room that adds onto the foundation, completing the master planned community that is "all there is."

At this point, we have to give props here to one of our favorite physicists, and one of the grandfathers of quantum physics, David Bohm. A protégé of Einstein, Bohm writes in *Wholeness and the Implicate Order* that the nature of reality is an unbroken whole that has three specific orders that worked together to create reality. The first level is the super-implicate order, which acts as an overseeing, creative, and generative order. The second level is the implicate order, which is the invisible process by which nothing becomes something. Beneath physical reality, consciousness and matter enfold in preparation for the third level. In the third order, the explicate order, the implicate is unfolded into physical reality.

The hidden world of the implicate may work somewhat like a hologram, which is projected from a higher dimensional reality onto our lower, three-dimensional reality. Each region of space-time would contain within it the image of the whole, like a hologram, and thus also contain the "enfolded" whole of reality within it. Another way of putting it is that any independent element in our universe contains with it the sum of all elements. The One contains the All. Bohm called this process the "holomovement," which is the ultimate reality.

THE HOLOGRAPHIC UNIVERSE

Think of the film *The Matrix,* perhaps in a less sinister sense, and you have an idea of the invisible infrastructure of this implicate order, where the actions occur by which the unmanifest become manifest. It almost sounds religious, and certainly metaphysical, which is why Bohm has become a scientific darling of the metaphysical world. He not only helped shape quantum mechanics, but also the idea that consciousness was a driver of the implicate and the enfolding of matter into the unfoldment of objects in the physical realm of reality.

The holographic principle was first proposed in 1993 by the Dutch physicist Gerard 't Hooft and the coinventor of string theory, Leonard Susskind. The principle stated that all basic information found in one region of our universe could be the equivalent of information found at our universe's boundary, similar to how our bodies project shadows onto the sidewalk.

In his book *The Holographic Universe: The Revolutionary Theory of Reality,* Michael Talbot examines the work that David Bohm did with Stanford University neurophysiologist Dr. Karl Pribram, who had his own similar theory about the holographic brain. The way the brain stores data through its entire volume is similar to the idea of enfoldment, and the idea that the entire universe might be contained in every small nook and cranny, even something as small as a blade of grass or grain of sand. Similarly, one region of the brain may encompass all the memory and data of the entire brain, and that memory may be "stored" elsewhere outside the brain and projected onto it. The holographic principle also posits that our universe may be nothing more than a two-dimensional projection upon our cosmological horizon, perceived as a three-dimensional reality at the macroscopic scale.

Talbot also brings the mind and consciousness into the mix, suggesting that we may be creating the holographic image of reality that is then projected onto the lower dimensional plane, or that we have something to do with how our reality is perceived and experienced. These ghostly projected images may also help to explain some of the more paranormal events people encounter, such as ghosts, UFOs, out-of-body experiences (OBEs), near-death experiences (NDEs), visions, and psychic abilities. Talbot states, "There is evidence to suggest that our world and everything in it . . . are also only ghostly images, projections from a level of reality so beyond our own it is literally beyond both space and time."

To think you could hold a small pebble in your hand and in a way hold the entire universe in your palm is the stuff of metaphysics, religion, and spirituality, but this principle posits just such a thing. Maybe the level of the Grid we live on is really just a projected image from somewhere else, where the original image has been imprinted and enfolded. It unfolds here, before our five senses, allowing us to experience it. But what about other images being projected on other parts of the Grid? Could we somehow be getting glimpses of those in the form of anomalous or paranormal phenomena? We will examine this possibility in chapter 6.

To imagine a finite number of levels is difficult, just as it is difficult to imagine a finite length to our universe. What lies beyond the edge? Perhaps with the Grid, the topmost level circles back around to the bottommost level, like the zero-point field, where all and nothing exists, waiting to be manifested.

Believing in levels of reality is not just a scientific concept but also one that has permeated all religious belief and tradition, again suggesting a hierarchy of worlds that a human being can experience, possibly over the course of many, many lifetimes. The Grid is where science and spirit and the supernatural all come together.

Reality isn't all it seems, or all we see.

CHAPTER 3

MANY MANSIONS

The Ancient and Religious History of the Grid

Heaven is under our feet as well as over our heads.
—HENRY DAVID THOREAU, *WALDEN*

Deep inside the fabric of matter and energy, there are gods and goddesses in embryo. Waiting to be born.
—DEEPAK CHOPRA, *THE SEVEN SPIRITUAL LAWS OF SUCCESS*

In my Father's house are many mansions: if it were not so, I would have told you. I go to prepare a place for you.
—JOHN 14:2

If science is about the structure of the universe, then spirituality is about the essence. We can never really understand the nature of reality unless we find a theory that encompasses both the implicate and the explicate. The microcosm and the macrocosm. As above, so below. The inside and the outside.

Dorothy couldn't understand Oz until she saw what, or who, was behind the curtain pressing the buttons and pulling the strings. Whether or not we believe in anything spiritual or religious, we can certainly appreciate the depth of wisdom of ancient religious traditions whose writers and creators pondered the same questions about the universe they were observing as we do today. From the dawn of recorded history, humans have whispered of what lies behind the curtain, beneath the shrouded veil of everyday reality. Beyond the door of ordinary perception and experience. They wondered about how it all worked, what laws were present, and what fundamental truths governed the movement of the stars and planets and even the atoms that make up all matter.

Cosmic Codes

The physicist Heinz Pagels said, "I think the universe is a message written in code, a cosmic code, and the scientist's job is to decipher that code. This idea, that the universe is a message, is very old." This code is the Grid in action, and it is not a new idea born of quantum physics theory or laws of modern science. It is an idea as old as time itself.

Creation myths and stories from a variety of cultures speak of a void of "nothingness," or a sea or field of vibrating energy from which everything comes and may one day return. This fundamental level of reality is the source and everything exists in this level, and yet nothing exists at all, simply because it has not yet been given physicality.

From the ancient primary texts of the Hindu Vedas, the Christian New Testament, and even the cosmogenesis stories and myths of the Sumerians, Babylonians, and ancient Egyptians, creation is said to come from a formless void containing the building blocks of life and physical existence, and this void or field (or Grid) permeates every inch of space-time. Think of the Kingdom of Heaven of the New Testament, described in the Gospel of Thomas as a formless field that is "inside you and outside you . . . spread out upon the Earth, but . . . men do not see it."

The levels of the Grid are implicate . . . and invisible, but somehow the whole of the Grid must have an origin point, one level from which the other levels spring forth when nothingness is acted upon by the forces of creation to manifest physical objects, matter, and form. To scientists, this could be the origin of sound and light itself that then, via some mechanism such as vibration or resonance, was utilized to give form to energy and matter. This sounds like the zero-point field of quantum physics, a field of superposition and potentiality that serves as a ground state for all matter. It is from this level that we come and to this level that we return, as we too are made up of particles vibrating at different frequencies, just like the "stuff" in the ZPF.

For many cultures and traditions, this level of reality was the primordial waters or the soup from which the chemical and biological reactions occurred to form life. In Egyptian creation myths, this primal field of the waters of life was called *Nun,* and all matter and form came from this infinite field. Nun was often called the Father of the Gods and was said to permeate every inch of space and time.

Many Eastern traditions would refer to this as the Supreme Mind or Supreme Consciousness, the force behind all physical manifestation. The Tibetan Book of the Dead speaks of realms of higher dimensions or divisions within as *bardo* ("intermediate state"). The seat of the gods is within us as unlimited dimensions or realms of reality. Hopi Native Americans in the Southwest believe there is a force behind form and physical manifestation called the heart of the cosmos, just as the Mandaeans in Iraq speak of a supreme and formless entity that expresses itself through both spiritual and physical creation. This parallels as well the fourth century BCE Chinese philosophy of the Tao Te Ching, which describes a void that is featureless yet complete, and born before heaven and Earth, thus implying three separate levels of reality (much like David Bohm's superimplicate, implicate, and explicate orders).

THINGS COME IN THREES

The concept of three levels of reality or process levels by which reality is manifested is common throughout many religious traditions, myths, and folklore. Going back to primitive traditions that emerged into shamanism, we have the three worlds by which shamans or medicine healers could journey to retrieve souls, heal the sick, and gain access to vital information from spirit and animal guides. These worlds, which are mirrored in many Native American traditions, consist of the upper world, the middle world, and the lower world.

The upper world is the home of higher beings, angels, and spirit guides with wisdom and information not accessible on the lower levels. This is where the teachers of humans exist, ready to impart their knowledge to the shaman who has journeyed there, usually to the rhythmic sounds of drumming and rattling designed to facilitate an altered state of consciousness.

The middle world mirrors everyday reality.

The lower world consists of power animals and archetypal forces that are more aligned with the instinctual and the subconscious. This is also the realm where the shaman can access the ancestral spirits of those they're trying to help.

A world tree serves as a center point to the entirety of creation, linking together the lower world, middle world, and upper world. The world tree is also said to be all of creation itself, much like the holographic universe, where each piece contains the entire universe within it.

Norse mythology recognizes three levels as well, divided into nine worlds:

- The upper level (the gods, the elves, and Vanir)
- The middle level (humans, giants, dark-elves, dwarves)
- The lower level (fire, the realm of the dead)

The world tree, here called the *Yggdrasil,* links these three levels.

Figure 3. The Russian World Tree, Yggdrasil. *Artist unknown/Public Domain*

The Aborigines also recognize an invisible world of the spiritual, which is often accessed during Dreamtime. Like shamans, they journey to another reality as "real" as the day-to-day one of normal existence. In Dreamtime, it is possible to communicate and interact with spirits, ancients, and ancestors, and the physical world is thought to be a manifestation of the activities of the spirit beings in the Dreaming. The Aboriginal cosmology embraces the understanding of both the spiritual and physical as interpenetrating parts of the whole of existence. They instinctually and intuitively know that the seen reality is not the only one and that other realities are equally important. The Great Father was the source from which all was created, and from the chaos order was given through the spirit beings that formed the physical landscape through the Dreaming.

This concept of a powerful creator or creative force emerging out of nothingness is found in most creation myths. Through a series of progressive events, the creator gives birth to gods and goddesses or beings responsible for the manifestation of the physical world. Everything is infused with the Divine force or breath or spirit, and creation begins from the point of this singular moment. Before then, there is nothing; after there is everything. The big bang of myth in all its varied forms starts, and ends, the same way.

The whole purpose of myth and creation stories is to give order and meaning to the universe, based on common scientific knowledge of the time, which is why these primal stories contain nuggets of truth and even some good, hard science hidden within the fictional contexts of how the world appeared to their uninitiated eyes. In *The Universal Myths: Heroes, Gods,*

Tricksters and Others, Alexander Eliot talks about the common elements of all global myths as a way for humans to wrap their minds around the creation of the world, and their role in it: "For members of archaic and traditional societies, myth narrates a sacred history, telling of events that took place in primordial time, the fabulous time of the 'beginnings.'" Myths are accounts of creation, and surprisingly all myths contain similar imagery and ideas as to how that creation came about.

These same myths recognized that all of nature, and reality, did not exist solely in the seen, but also the unseen. Eliot writes, "The kind of intelligence which creates mythologies is that which recognizes the presence of enormous and incomprehensible forces hidden away in the depths of nature—of worlds within worlds and beyond all the worlds that are directly known to us." Chief deities and gods and goddesses often existed in or presided over these unseen realms of reality, their effects and influences felt in the natural world as weather, earthquakes, volcanic activity, and the cycles of plant and animal life. What man could control in his level of the Grid, the higher beings controlled from their thrones in the heavens, imparting their star knowledge to humans only when they saw fit to do so.

Meanwhile, humans on Earth had to make sense of the rules and actions of the gods and their hidden worlds. Religion and myth served as a means for creating order out of such disorder, and understanding out of the unknown and unknowable.

The great religions of the East and the West had their own levels or realms of existence. *Trailokya* is the "three realms," or worlds, of early Buddhist cosmology. Also described as planes or dimensions of existence, they relate to the principles of karma and karmic rebirth and the brahmanical fourfold world concept of four different levels of reality much like the Judeo-Christian heaven, hell and purgatory:

Brahmanical Worlds	Buddhist Worlds
Bhur, the earth realm	Kamadhatu, the world of desire
Bhuvah, the heavenly realm	Rupadhatu, the world of form
Swar, the sky realm	Arupadhatu, the formless world
Mahar, the eternal	

The Hindu Puranas ("of ancient times") are ancient texts which describe fourteen realms that are divided into seven higher heavens and seven lower heavens. Lord Vishnu, the Supreme God of Hinduism, lives in the highest of the heavens. Earth exists in the lowest of the seven higher heavens. The lower realms are the underworlds. All are called *lokas,* the Sanskrit word for "worlds," which in the Veda consisted of a triple world, or trailokya, like the Buddhist three realms, divided into earth, sky, and heaven. This was the universe of Vedic thought.

The Tao, the Way, of Lao Tzu tells us: "There is a thing, formless yet complete. Before heaven and earth it existed. We do not know its name, but we call it Tao. It is the mystery of the mysteries." This ancient Chinese philosophical system uses the sacred writings of the Tao Te Ching and the Zhuangzi to formulate a tradition that focuses on the path or way to action through non-action and the Three Treasures of compassion, moderation, and humility.

The Tao is based on the concept of the attainment of the Way and the understanding that the Tao can be found everywhere, from the lowliest to the highest. There is no place the Tao is not: "The power that makes things what they are doesn't have the limitation that belongs to things, and when we speak of things being limited, we mean that they're bounded in themselves. The Tao is the limit of the unlimited, and the boundlessness of the unbounded." We hate to keep bringing it up, but the Tao sounds an awful lot like the Grid, or the totality of the unlimited, even with its inclusion of the limited.

In the Tao, the energy present everywhere that makes all form, matter, substance is called *chi*. Remember the zero-point energy that permeates every inch of "empty space"? The influential fourth century BCE philosopher Chuang Tzu describes the Tao as such: "It has both reality and substance, but it does nothing and has no material form . . . Before there was Heaven and Earth, from of old, there it was, eternally existing . . . it fills Heaven and Earth and envelops everything within the Universe." Like the Kingdom of Heaven of the New Testament, the Tao is everywhere and anywhere, all through us and all around us, and yet we cannot see it. It has no physical form. It is a hidden infrastructure of reality upon which everything seen and physical and manifest is built.

SOME-THING FROM NO-THING

The Western religious traditions of Judaism and Christianity adopted a similar notion of creation coming from nothing, a void into which God spoke and then created light and form and living things. Judeo-Christianity also recognizes the tri-level reality of heaven, hell, and purgatory/Earth, which may have originally symbolized the higher spirit world, ordinary reality, and instinctual, survival-based existence. Some more metaphysically leaning writers and teachers equate heaven, Earth, and hell with spirit/soul, mind, and body. The body is not evil or "hellish," but rather the most basic and fundamental level of survival, the instinctual and primal. The mind represents the earthly realm where the body is able to express itself. Heaven is the realm of the spirit and soul and all forms of higher thought, intention, and consciousness.

In the Talmud, we find seven heavens called *shamayim* that make up the Judaic concept of the universe, with the throne of the Lord located at the highest of the seven realms. The number seven is found in many religious and sacred texts, as it represents completion. In Islamic thought, the number seven may also have corresponded to the knowledge of seven celestial bodies (other than Earth) at the time: the sun, the moon, Mercury, Venus, Mars, Jupiter, and Saturn. It would make sense that what was in the heavens was mirrored in the stories of sacred texts. As above, so below.

The Kabbalah teaches of the Ein Sof, which is God before manifest form. From the Ein Sof emanate different realms through which God expresses and creates, each an aspect of the Divine. These are the ten sefirot (also spelled sephirot) of the Kabbalistic Tree of Life. Again notice the tree motif, which

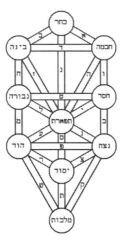

Figure 4. The Kabbalistic Tree of Life or Sefirot. *Courtesy of PuckSmith/Public Domain*

The Grid

serves as the unifier of the cosmos. These ten sefirot were said to have emanated into the cosmic womb in order to create the universe. Something from nothing, manifest made from unmanifest. Levels of reality that begin with a foundational source or field or void or primal soup from which all of physical nature is given form.

The ten sefirot, in descending order, consist of:

- Keter (the crown)
- Chokhmah (wisdom)
- Binah (intuition, understanding)
- Chesed (mercy) or Gedulah (greatness)
- Gevurah (strength)
- Tiferet (glory)
- Netzach (victory)
- Hod (majesty)
- Yesod (foundation)
- Malkut (sovereignty)

These qualities of God are often divided into four realms or worlds by some modern Kabbalah practitioners—the Divine, the Creative, the Formative, and the Physical—and given the name *olam* to mean different dimensions or levels of reality that are all part of the greater Tree of Life. Each of the four worlds is governed by a different angel or entity or hierarchy of entities. These four levels of reality remind us of Bohm's orders, with the superimplicate working on the implicate through the "holomovement," which is the process of the enfolding and then the unfolding of the explicate into physical reality.

The ten sefirot are a part of the Ein Sof, again as if part of a hologram. The creation of all from empty space is referred to in some Kabbalistic traditions as a withdrawal of God into itself to create a void from which all manifestation comes forth. This may sound a bit like the big bang of physics, where the known (and possibly unknown) universe sprang out of nothing that then became a tiny point, imploding inward then expanding outward. In the Zohar, the foundational text of the Kabbalah, we learn, "Before He gave shape to the world, before He produced any form, He was alone, without form and without resemblance to anything else." Perhaps this was the state of superposition of quantum physics. Science and religion often speak the same language, albeit using different terminology.

The Tree of Life and sefirot of the Kabbalah are surprisingly similar to the Egyptian Tree of Life and the Kemetic Tree of Life, both of which were said to have influenced later Kabbalistic thought. Kemetism is a form of ancient Egyptian paganism that is found in many African tribal traditions. In fact, the concept of the ten-point Kemetic Tree of Life is thought to have African origins, representing the cosmos as expressed and manifested by the goddesses or gods of each appropriate tradition.

GLOBAL SYMBOLOGY

Why do so many of the world's religious traditions have the same imagery, iconography, concepts, beliefs, and understandings of the seen and the unseen? Why do so many of the origin stories talk of the same primal soup, or void, or nothingness, from which manifest reality comes? Why does this occult understanding of the presence of a hidden infrastructure of reality, the Grid itself, permeate all belief systems regardless of how sophisticated or primitive the culture?

In the Qur'an, the holy text of Islam, seven heavens layered one above the other are part of the unseen universe and hidden order, as well as the visible universe around us. This description of heaven does not align necessarily with the "paradise" of Judeo-Christian thought, but instead is the expanse of all realities where angels and spirits abide. The ultimate level of heaven is the realm of the Divine Throne, where the Almighty who created the seven heavens is seated.

In Shi'ite Islamic tradition, the seven heavens are divided into three sections, the lowest, middle, and highest, much like in shamanism and native tradition. The idea of three realms of existence is popular with a variety of cultures and traditions, but may have been the most simplistic way of expressing an understanding of the multiverse or other realities without the benefit of modern physics and scientific terminology. These levels may be "consciousness" or mental levels of experienced reality, but they may also be real, physical worlds that can occasionally be accessed by whatever means necessary. Shamans may not physically leave the spot they are sitting on when they journey to the upper world, and yet a part of them may enter another reality that is quite real.

Experiencing the Grid does not always mean bringing your body with you. In fact, even the great philosophers suggest different levels of reality exist, though they're talking more about the mental kind than the physical. Plato, the classical Greek philosopher, mathematician, and student of Socrates, imagined there were four levels of reality involving forms, which were timeless and transcendental and existed independent of human consciousness. These levels begin with the lowest level of illusion based on external appearances and beliefs. The next level is informed awareness, which serves to distinguish ordinary reality through sensible objects. The third level of lower forms involves deduction and reasoning, and the highest level involves a reality where we move beyond the deductive to the realm of direct knowing and understanding. These realities are more mental, but they still apply to how we view, perceive, and experience the "outer" reality and other hidden realities.

Other forms of philosophy recognize levels of reality that are similar, beginning with the level of physical forms, the level that we humans live in with objects we can perceive and touch and see. Then there is the quantum level, the world of the invisible activity of the subatomic, where particles pop in and out of existence, determining what will be manifested into physical form on a grander scale. And then there is the cosmic level of the universal, on a scale so awesome we may never know the full extent of it. There may also be a fourth level of angels, beings, and spirits that operates beyond the veils of perception.

As Above, So Below

The Egyptian-Greek Hermetic texts from the second and third centuries CE proclaim "as above, so below," that what occurs at the macrocosmic level also occurs at the microcosmic. In *The Emerald Tablet of Hermes Trismegistus,* one of the tracts of the greater teachings known as the Hermetica, there are three levels of reality: physical, emotional, and mental, and what happens in one influences the other two. The microcosmic individual self then mirrors the macrocosmic universal, and vice versa, and Hermes stated that an understanding of the workings of one led to understanding of the other. We are walking universes, tiny holographic slivers of the greater hologram projected onto the cosmic landscape.

The great Hermes, who wrote the wisdom teachings between the second and third centuries BCE, believed that all existed in the mind of God, Atum, and that everything was an idea in the mind. Atum is continuously creating creation, everything beginning as a thought in the Divine mind. Atum is Primal Mind, described as "the Supreme Absolute Reality, filled with ideas which are imperceptible to the senses, and with all-embracing knowledge." Hermes believed that all things were thoughts, which the Atum thinks, including the cosmos and man.

Interestingly enough, Atum is born out of a big bang of a cry from the turbulent depths of the womb of space, and the light or mind of God emerges and speaks a word to calm the chaotic waters. This first word serves as the beginning of a blueprint or infrastructure by which the ideas of the mind of God will be made into the manifest cosmos. In the beginning there was the light, and the word—sound familiar?

Atum is "hidden, yet obvious everywhere." He is the root and the source of all. Atum is the whole, which contains everything. The All and the One are identical. The Kingdom of Heaven . . . the zero-point field . . . the holographic universe . . . the Grid.

So we have an image, a vision, of this Grid. But how does it work?

Part Two

Connectors, Triggers, and Mechanisms of the Grid

CHAPTER 4

GETTING FROM HERE TO THERE

External Connectors, Triggers, and Mechanisms in the Grid

The dance goes from realizing that you're separate (which is the awakening) to then trying to find your way back into the totality of which you are not only a part, but which you are.

—RAM DASS

Reality . . . is pictured as a limitless series of levels which extend to deeper and deeper subtleties and out of which the particular, explicate order of nature and the order of consciousness and life emerge.

—F. DAVID PEAT, SYNCHRONICITY

What does it matter if there are multiple realities and many worlds if we cannot access them? To actually witness another level of the Grid is what we live for, what we aspire to.

Let's go back to the skyscraper imagery, of floors that are connected to one another by elevators, escalators, fire escapes, and staircases. These connectors allow a person to move between floors and experience what "reality" is on each level of the building.

In the hidden infrastructure of the Grid, there are similar connectors. These are means by which the natural world allows us to move up and down, side to side, and in between. Some of them are even the stuff of science fiction bordering on fact; that is, they are theoretically possible.

We begin with wormholes.

Wormholes: A Connector between Levels of the Grid

A wormhole is nothing more than a black hole at one end and a white hole at the other end. A white hole is a black hole "exit point" for the potential tunnel. Just imagine a big red apple (or green if you are into Granny Smiths) and a worm crawling along the outside. The worm wants to get to the other side, and he has two choices: The long way around involves going along the exterior of the apple. But

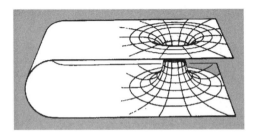

Figure 5. A wormhole can connect two points in one universe or parallel universes. *Courtesy of ScienceForum/Wikimedia Commons*

the worm can, if he's strong enough, bore right through the middle of the apple and get there faster.

Similarly, theoretical and quantum physicists point to wormholes as potential shortcuts between points in the space-time continuum. These points may be within the same universe, or they may link parallel universes so that a wormhole begins in Universe A but may end up in Universe L or

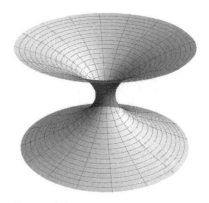

Figure 6. Lorentzian traversable wormholes allow travel in both directions from one part of the universe to another part, or travel between universes. *Courtesy of Allen McC/Wikimedia Commons*

M or R or Z. Wormholes can also be shortcuts in time, such as past to present, future to past, and so on.

The term wormhole was coined way back in 1957 by physicist John Archibald Wheeler, but the theory itself had been around long before, evident in the works of German mathematicians Bernhard Riemann, Felix Klein, Adolf Hurwitz, Hermann Weyl, and others, and in the research of Albert Einstein and Nathan Rosen, who proposed the Einstein-Rosen Bridge as a wormhole theory. German physicist Karl Schwarzschild became known for the traversable wormhole theory, called a Lorentzian wormhole, which again is basically a black hole entry with a white hole exit that connects two points via their horizons in either one universe or in parallel universes.

Modern day theoretical and quantum physicists such as Kip Thorne, Frank Tipler, Carl Sagan, Stephen Hawking, Michio Kaku, Lisa Randall, Brian Greene, and Fred Alan

Wolf (among many others) have introduced potentially viable ways to stabilize the throats of traversable wormholes, mainly via the use of as-yet-to-be-discovered exotic matter. This matter might offset the deadly gravitational pull at the mouth of the event horizon, the point at which nothing can escape the wormhole—not even light! This would allow the wormhole throat to stay open enough to allow for something to pass through the tunnel through time and space . . . and survive intact. It has not happened yet, but it is theoretically sound.

So if two points in the Grid are accessible via wormholes, might this allow space travelers from other civilizations the chance to visit us here on Earth? And might this also allow time travelers to visit us as well? The shortcut between universes may indeed be like an elevator between floors in a large building, with the ability to not only move from one floor to another in a spatial sense, but also travel forward and backward in time, just as an elevator can bring you *back* to a floor you already visited at any time. Just press the right button when you get in.

With these cosmic wormholes, we look to the time when an actual object can traverse safely through, but physicists also point to information utilizing wormholes as well. If information itself, the its and bits that make up the universe and all that inhabits it, can move between worlds, perhaps the potential then exists for the means by which life came about to be seeded elsewhere. Information may carry the fundamental basics for the physical laws that worked so well in our universe, and may then begin or evolve the same life processes in another universe. We want to believe that we can send a manned spaceship through a wormhole into another reality, but we may have to settle for what little its and bits of basic information we can get first to boldly go where no man or woman has gone before.

But are there wormholes right here on Earth? Do portals or doorways where entities and energy from one reality can transfer into our reality really exist? Vortices or hot spots where anomalies exist in the environment that allow for a thinning of the veil between worlds? Could these Earth-based wormholes even be the means of access for such things as ghosts, aliens, and cryptids?

There is no scientific proof that wormholes exist in space, let alone on our planet, but people do speak of "zones of high strangeness" where paranormal activity and UFO sightings are more populous than elsewhere, where all kinds of unusual experiences involving altered states of consciousness, energy shifts, and even slips in time have been reported. What else might account for the prevalence of "haunted" locales, or UFO hot spots where waves of sightings occur to numerous witnesses, or even places where strange creatures pop into and out of view right in front of terrified humans who could swear, as many reports suggest, they "came from nowhere and disappeared right back into it"?

If there are many levels of the Grid by which something can travel from here to there, and vice versa, must we accept that cosmic wormholes are the only theoretical connector? There are millions of people throughout the world who claim to have experienced or witnessed what we deem paranormal or anomalous activity, and much of it involves some type of energy or "being" that doesn't by normal standards exist here in our own reality on a regular basis. So maybe there are earthly connectors that allow for movement between floors of the infrastructure, elevators right here on our own planet that can serve as a means for getting from Point A to all other points available.

PORTALS AND POWER LINES

Sacred geometry suggests that we can amplify the mystical powers of nature by aligning buildings with certain points in the landscape. Ley lines are a popular and contentious topic involving straight lines that were once ancient travel routes or pathways yet were also given a spiritual significance related to the Chinese concept of feng shui. By aligning edifices and monuments in ancient times, one created a line of power, which symbolically mirrored the heavens here on Earth (remember, "as above, so below") and made sacred the buildings that dotted the path of the lines.

Even aligning a particular monument with stars or planets, or constellations and astronomical events, was thought to amplify a place's power and create an environment conducive to altered states of consciousness and the experience of other realms and worlds. Places like Stonehenge in Britain, Sedona in the Arizona desert, or the Giza pyramids of Egypt are still thought to be portals that, when the environmental aspects are in perfect alignment, somehow create a doorway to other realities. People trek by the thousands to such locales, hoping to have an experience that they feel they cannot achieve back home in less sacred Jersey or Cleveland (we beg to differ!).

A portal doesn't necessarily have to be in outer space or on land, though. The Bermuda Triangle and its sister spots, the Devil's Triangle in Japan and the Great Lakes Triangle in the United States, are three possible Earth-based wormholes. Located over bodies of water where decades worth of mysterious events have boggled the minds of researchers, debunkers and believers alike, these places share some interesting characteristics. Between these three locations alone, hundreds of ships, planes, and other craft have vanished. A few witnesses have returned to tell about electromagnetic anomalies that caused their controls to go haywire; the presence of a green "fog" that, once entered, proved to be a time slip mechanism; the sound of static electrical charges and bizarre weather that accompanied these near-disappearances; even UFO sightings have been reported!

We have no proof that any of these locations are anything more than normal, natural zones of strangeness that elude our understanding and lead to pilot error and disorientation. But we also have no proof that these are not actual locations where the external elements present create just the right foundation for objects, and people, to be sucked into other realities, never to be heard from again. When it comes to our environment, we tend to look at nature and its behavior in terms of what we perceive as our reality, but certain environmental effects may be behind experiences that go beyond our reality, beyond our perception, and even beyond our understanding.

While wormholes may be one connector of levels of the Grid, what are the triggers and mechanisms that might be involved right here on Earth that create them?

WATER: A TRIGGER AND MECHANISM THAT CREATES A CONNECTOR

Water itself may be an external trigger and mechanism, a culprit for the manifestation of anomalous experiences. When coupled with particulars of barometric pressure, temperature, and general weather conditions, water could be part of the necessary ingredients to create a wormhole, vortex, or portal, any of which would act as an opening to another energetic reality. Negative ions are found in increased levels near ocean waves and waterfalls, and before and after thunderstorms. The seashore contains about 50,000–100,000 negative ions per cubic centimeter, as opposed to an office room, which contains about 40–100. Research has shown that negative ions are associated with many physiological effects as well, but our focus right now is environmental.

In the Grid, we want to know what may be acting as connectors between realities, and perhaps the presence of water is a major connective force that allows for these openings to be created. In places of high strangeness like the Bermuda Triangle, could the presence of horrendous thunderstorms lead to an increase in negative ions, which may interact with the presence of ships and craft?

We know that water does not conduct electricity, but this only applies to pure water. Put an impurity in the water, like salt in the ocean, and when it is dissolved it separates into differently charged atoms, or ions. Salt ($NaCl$) breaks up into positive sodium (Na) ions and negative chlorine (Cl) ions. These ions float around and carry a charge, which can conduct electricity. If you were to place a battery with a negative pole into the water, the negative ions would be attracted to the positive pole, and the positive to the negative, creating a closed circuit.

Electromagnetic anomalies abound in places where people claim to have paranormal experiences. With the influences of water and ions and electricity, not to mention what might be going on above the sea with weather conditions such as air temperature, barometric pressure, and levels of humidity, the stew might be created for a passing ship or plane to fall prey to a rip in the space-time continuum, one right here on Earth.

This is pure conjecture, but think about the popular conception of haunted houses with thunder and lightning raging in the skies, or haunted ships like the Flying Dutchman appearing out of nowhere to those in the wrong place at the wrong time. Fluctuations in the electromagnetic field, caused and coupled by the presence of water, storms, and electricity sources such as lightning, may be the ingredients needed for a ghost or entity from another world to show up in ours.

Add to that the presence and physiological conditions of the observers, such as humans on a ghost-hunting tour, or the crew on a doomed ship, and you have the external and internal alignment of conditions required to access other levels of the Grid not ordinarily experienced in day-to-day life.

Electromagnetism (EM) has a long and interesting association with otherworldly phenomena, despite no real scientific reasoning. The evidence is circumstantial, thanks in part to the general presence of EM level fluctuations found in old buildings with exposed wiring and natural settings, such as supposedly haunted cemeteries and lighthouses. Most alleged haunted locales are not brand spanking new homes with solid and covered wiring, water sources deep underground, or nearby waterfalls or ocean waves that might influence the environmental conditions around the building.

Our own bodies give off EM fields, too, and may account for higher readings on simple measuring devices favored by ghost hunters (along with ion detectors), who often lack the knowledge of EM fields and the natural causes for high and low levels. Theories abound, including one that suggests the energy created by differences in pressure systems during a storm can create anomalous activity at a specific location. The significant pressure differences between air masses of different densities cause energy movement, and perhaps that movement is the key that unlocks the door to the Grid.

This theory does not explain why people experience anomalous activity on land far from water sources, and in perfect weather conditions, but there may be other external influences, such as the presence of seismic activity, infrasound, or ultrasound. In fact, there is a popular theory which suggests that water can retain an imprint of energies it has been exposed to. Perhaps this imprint may then manifest as ghostly activity. In 1988 French immunologist Dr. Jacques Benveniste published a paper in *Nature* that came to just such a conclusion. He conducted his research at the Aerospace Institute of the University of Stuttgart in Germany and came to the conclusion that water may contain not only the ability to imprint and then transfer vast amounts of information across distances, but that it may influence our own bodies as well (after all, we are mostly water!).

Also known as "digital biology," specific molecular audio signals called the "beat" frequencies of water's infrared vibrations may be collected, transmitted, and amplified to affect other water molecules nearby as receivers.

So, if water retains an imprint of the vibrational frequency of a past event, might it also retain ghosts? And might the presence of negative ions and/or electrical charges somehow serve to release those ghosts and allow them to be perceived by an observer nearby?

There is a similar theory called the Stone Tape Theory that allows for the same influences in dry spots, such as homes and buildings, where information can be imprinted on certain types of substrate materials such as walls and floors, and then later played back to observers present like a video or audio-tape in the form of ghostly apparitions and spooky voices and sounds. These apparitions are imprinted, so their behavior is always the same, because it truly is a recorded impression and not a real "ghost" strutting around. Sir William Barrett, a founding member of the Society for Psychical Research in the late nineteenth century, stated that "in certain cases of haunt-ings and apparitions, some kind of local imprint, on mate-rial structures or places, has been left by some past events occurring to certain persons, who when on Earth, lived or were closely connected to that particular locality; an echo or phantom of these events becoming perceptible to those now living."

More recently, Professors William A. Tiller and Walter Dibble, Jr., conducted experiments altering water chemistry with thought impressions and intentions (yes, you read that right, *thought and intentions*) and concluded that water was a special material that was able to transfer energy and infor-mation "from the intention domain onto the conventional domain of cognition." A similar experiment conducted in 1996 by Dr. David Schweitzer, grandson of Albert Schweitzer, photographed changes in minute particles of water as a result of thought influence. Using fluorescent microscopes, Schweitzer determined that water was acting as a liquid memory system that could actually store information.

If we go back to the zero-point field of the previous chapter, once again we are left with the feeling that energy and information are recorded onto an infinite field, or Grid, that is accessible when both external and internal influences offer a connection between the levels of reality.

Imprints are only one type of ghostly activity. Other ghost sightings involve entities that do not repeat actions and behaviors, and are often even aware they are being observed. Parallel universe anyone? Gridwalkers, indeed.

Infrasound

In addition to EM fluctuations, which occur both on land and over water, there is also sound to contend with . . . mainly infrasound. The range of human hearing is between 20 hertz (Hz) and 20,000 Hz. Infrasound is below our range of hearing, 20 Hz and below, and has been linked to a variety of physiological effects, such as disorientation, nausea, headaches, and even the sense of not being alone or of a presence or shadow figure nearby. We know this thanks to the infrasound experimentation of Nikola Tesla, Vic Tandy, and Michael Persinger. Infrasound increases in conjunction with major storms, volcanic eruptions, and seismic activity, and because infrasound travels faster through water and solids without dissipation, it could possibly be linked to an increase in anomalous phenomena. And not just because of how it affects the environment, but also because of how it affects our own physical bodies as well. Out in the oceans, where the greatest storms rage, and under the sea, the Earth's plates move and groan and the conditions are ripe for anything . . . for the lucky, or unlucky, soul that happens to be present at the time.

Infrasound also increases with the presence of auroras and EM fluctuations, solar activity, particular rocket launches, supersonic jets, meteors, nuclear explosions, air flow over mountains, and even avalanches. We don't even need to add water to get the right elements for a potential Grid level connection.

A popular theory involving animal reactions to oncoming earthquakes posits that many species are responding to the infrasonic waves that occur prior to a big shock, as the Earth's massive plates begin to move and rub against each other. Ultrasound, which is also outside our hearing range, is heard easily by creatures such as bats and might also play a role in anomalous activity. But few if any studies have tested the influences of ultrasound on human physiology. Ultrasound is responsible for echolocation in many animal species, and indeed influences nature, even if we cannot feel or sense that influence ourselves.

There is so much we humans cannot see or hear that to even imagine what we might not be aware of on this level of the Grid only leads to even greater imaginings as to what other levels may hold. There may be ranges of vision and hearing available in these other levels that we cannot *even* imagine, and creatures and entities that utilize these ranges that are but a mystery to our eyes and ears. Our reality is so limited, perhaps as a survival mechanism that allows us to do what is necessary to function here on this level. But we do get those wonderful glimpses all the time of other realities, and even other aspects of our own reality that sometimes evade our understanding. Spend a day in nature with no watch or clocks and time takes on a whole different behavior. Watch animals in their natural setting and see that they react to things in the air, around them, and underneath them that we don't perceive. Ever watch a cat come into a room, look up in the air with terror, and run out again? Did *you* see what the cat saw??

Maybe there are places all around us on this reality that we cannot even perceive yet, let alone other realities, and all that would be required is a tweaking of some environmental aspect. If only we knew which ones. For all we know, the doorways and portals could be everywhere.

But we are called upon to look at why so much of the activity deemed paranormal does occur in certain "hot spot" settings, and why there are indeed places on or near major bodies of water where things vanish into thin air, never to be seen again. If the entire planet were one massive wormhole, or crawling with smaller such shortcuts to other worlds, we would have a hard time existing safely in this one! But what if there are places where all the factors required fall into place to serve as the elevators between levels of the Grid? And why are certain individuals able to perceive these paranormal or anomalous events and not others? More to come on that. But first, speaking of vibrational frequencies, the next potential connector, which also can serve as a trigger/mechanism, is resonance.

Resonance: A Connector and Trigger

Quantum physics tells us that nothing is solid. Everything at its most fundamental level vibrates, resonates with its own frequency. String theory is based on this same concept that everything is made up of vibrating strings of various resonances, open and closed and looped. At the bottom level of the Grid, there is nothing but vibration and potentiality, before some unseen force assigns form. That which is formless is given form by an underlying vibration. Werner Heisenberg, the Nobel Prize–winning German physicist, once posited "the ontology of materialism rested upon the illusion that the kind of existence, the direct 'actuality' of the world around us, can be extrapolated into the atomic range. This extrapolation, however, is impossible. Atoms are not things." No, they are not fixed and measurable things at all at their most fundamental level. They are vibrations and potentialities awaiting the act of observation to fix them into form.

Resonance is described simply as the tendency of a particular system to oscillate with greater amplitude at some frequencies than others. Resonance is the effect, therefore, that is created when the natural vibrational frequency of one object, form, or body is amplified by the reinforcing vibrations of another object, form, or body, especially when those two things have near the exact same frequency. Think of being in a guitar shop and strumming a chord on one guitar. The other untouched guitars nearby will begin to emit that same vibrational chord. Particular vibratory frequencies can sync and form greater amplitude. The maximum amount of amplitude a particular frequency within a system can respond to is called the resonant frequency. Particles may have a resonant frequency, and entire systems such as the human body, even the Earth itself, have a range of resonant frequencies.

A wonderful example of resonance at work is the shattering wineglass courtesy of an opera singer's high note. The perfect pitch and resonance of the note match that of the glass, and you have a big mess to clean up. Or think of a swing set at the playground. If you push too hard, your child goes flying off the swing. If you push too softly, your child complains and whines. But push just right, and the force and motion are in perfect resonance with the swing, and your child has a wonderful time.

There are various types of resonance, such as mechanical, acoustic, quantum wave functioning, nuclear magnetic, and electromagnetic, and resonance can occur naturally as well as in manmade devices. Harmonics is a collection of resonances that create music. Harmonics that are in phase or in sync produce lovely chords or resonances. Those that are out of phase or sync produce dissonance or discord. When two or more notes are played together, you end up with something that either sounds good or sounds awful. This is the concept behind sympathetic vibratory physics, proposed by physicist and natural philosopher Walter Russell in *A New Concept of the Universe.* This is also the implicate vibratory world of David Bohm's enfolding into unfolding, nothing into something. Matter and form vibrate their way there.

For the purposes of the Grid, we need to focus on the fact that the most fundamental level of existence is *not solid.* The Grid itself is a vibration structure, as is everything within it.

There are several existing theories that posit that when vibratory frequencies are synced, some kind of "opening" or opportunity is created whereby energy can transfer from system to system. Imagine two universes parallel to one another, and various resonances occur between these universes that may allow for the cross communication of energy and information, even possibly the cross travel of actual forms and beings.

When resonance is created between various present frequencies, the resulting vibration creates its own new resonant frequency and may be the connecting doorway to whole new worlds and realities. We wrote extensively about resonance and its influences on everything from day-to-day reality to health and healing to the paranormal in our book *The Resonance Key: Exploring the Links between Vibrations, Consciousness, and the Zero Point Grid.* To us, resonance is the key to so many aspects of how we get something from the sea of nothingness known as the void, the field, the Grid. It takes a concerted decision to sync resonant frequencies to create new energy, matter, form, and we will explore what may be behind that concerted decision. But because everything vibrates at its simplest level, it isn't until these vibrations connect with each other and amplify into mass and form and physicality that we actually have something tangible to call reality. Perhaps by the simple act of observation we may be the ones collapsing the wave functions of this sea of quantum resonance into fixed and measurable objects vibrating in close synchronization with one another. Thus we have a chair, a dog, a computer, and a sock with its match missing.

Physicist Claude Swanson wrote about the synchronization between realities and the potential cross talk of information and energy in his book *The Synchronized Universe,* which lays out his vision of universes like sheets, one lying atop the other but not necessarily touching, with resonance as the key between them. When frequencies are synced, there is a connection between the two universes by which information and energy can move in and out. Because nothing exists in nature other than vibration, we can only imagine how many of these connections may occur naturally, even without our interference or knowledge, out of which and into which things flow.

The connectors between levels of the Grid may not always allow for interaction between all levels, perhaps just between two or six or eleven. It depends on the resonance occurring between levels, which may or may not happen very often; thus, the very fleeting nature of experiences we call "unreal" or "otherworldly." Resonant syncing is not consistent or even predictable yet, but we may be able to walk the Grid by matching our own vibrational frequencies with the experiences we desire or intend to have. This requires another mechanism: consciousness.

But before we swim that river, we go back to the idea that resonance acts as a main connector between floors in the skyscraper, or levels in the Grid. Earlier we looked at various external/environmental influences that could alter our perception or experience of reality, or open an Earth-based wormhole or portal between worlds. Combined with elements such as the presence of infrasound, electromagnetic fluctuations, or negative ions (or even positive ions!) and the weather and presence of water and electrical charges in the atmosphere, seismic activity, or any other number of environmental influences, the vibratory nature of reality itself would be changed.

These factors, alone or combined in any way, along with our physiology, which we tackle in the next chapter, may be the triggers and mechanisms by which connectors like resonance can work. The triggers and mechanisms operate along with the connectors to create a new environment, a new energy, a new opportunity, for anything, formed and formless, to move from level to level to level.

THE FIELD

There is another connector we must discuss: the "nature" of the Grid—the field. Various field theories, such as the zero-point field, propose that there is an infinite and invisible field that is the void from which all things rise and are given form. This unmanifested field is a dumping ground for everything that ever was and will be in terms of information, energy, and matter. Even thought exists here, and time, too. Past, present, and future all exist at once in a landscape that can be walked and traveled through—well, if you know the right roads to take.

The field aspect of the Grid is also its fundamental level, yet when broken down to even smaller parts we find resonance and vibration. So perhaps this field is a whole of resonance that contains all potential vibratory nature. There have been so many names for this field level . . . logos, the Matrix, the zero-point field, the Higgs field, the akasha, the primal void. As a connector, what we must do is find again the triggers and mechanisms by which we can move about the field and access the levels of the Grid. Again, we propose that even though the field itself is a connector, it may require actions taken on behalf of other connectors, such as resonance, to navigate.

The Grid is a web, and as we walk along that web we simply search for those connectors using the triggers and mechanisms we have at our disposal to jump from one strand to another.

The field is not the Grid in its entirety, but it permeates it, as the Kingdom of Heaven of the New Testament is in and through all things. The field, the Matrix, is the inherent structure of the thing, but not the thing itself. It may be only one level of the thing itself, because we cannot begin to imagine the physical laws that make up other stopping points along the Grid. Our reality is fixed in such a way that we often cannot ponder other realities that obey other natural laws.

Perhaps extra dimensions of space and time are required to move about the field level, as posited by Rupert Sheldrake in *Morphic Resonance: The Nature of Formative Causation.* Sheldrake's theory of morphic fields is similar to Bohm's concept of the implicate order and the vacuum field of quantum physics. Sheldrake, a former research fellow of the Royal Society, used his rich background in biochemistry and cell biology at Cambridge University to develop his theory that morphogenetic fields are behind the forms and organizations of biological, chemical, and physical systems, and that the effects and influences of these are visible in nature. He says, "These fields order the systems with which they are associated by affecting events that, from an energetic point of view, appear to be indeterminate or probabilistic; they impose patterned restrictions on the energetically possible outcomes of physical processes." Sheldrake then goes on to say that if these morphogenetic fields are responsible for the organization and form of material systems, they first must have characteristic structures. He suggests these field structures are "derived from the morphogenetic fields associated with previous similar systems; the morphogenetic fields of all past systems become present to any subsequent similar system; the structures of past systems affect subsequent similar systems by a cumulative influence that acts across both space and time." Thus, the systems are organized almost out of habit, because they were done that way before. This field theory is based on the idea that the level of formative causation is influenced by the characteristics of what came before, rather than the introduction of new characteristics.

This somewhat mirrors the regenerative nature of the zero-point field, which adds back into itself the ongoing snowballing collective of present events and forms into the existing field of the past. It also sounds similar to Ervin Laszlo's akashic field, which retains a sense of "cosmic memory" and the entirety of the past, present, and future. Laszlo states that akashic experiences of oneness and nonmaterial connectivity are examples of this cosmic memory field, which allows for the transmitting of information across the vast landscape of space and time. This cosmic memory information is not accessible via ordinary experience or through our five senses. Information is key here, because it is the "stuff" of experience itself.

Physicist John Wheeler once said that the most fundamental feature of our universe is information, and the other physical qualities are all incidentals. As Laszlo points out, "Information is present throughout space and time, and it is present at the same time everywhere." Information is recorded, conserved, and conveyed via this fundamental field, or unified field (it doesn't matter what you call it), that underlies and manifests all of the things and processes of the universe.

Thus, the language of the field, and the language of the Grid, is information. It is the communicative stuff of the ether, the substrate, the rock-bottom level of existence and reality.

Laszlo states that the akashic field is made up of "multidimensional realms" and that a number of anomalous and paranormal experiences can be accounted for in this field. Because it involves moving between realms of realities, with cross talk between realms occurring under particular environmental and physiological circumstances, anyone can move about the akasha and travel back to the past, into the future, and across vast spatial landscapes and benefit from the information and memory components present in this unified field. In the foreword to the book *The Way of the Explorer,* former astronaut and visionary Edgar Mitchell describes this experience as of the "first sense" and not the sixth sense, as if this is our most basic sense of perception and experience.

These similarities in field theories are as exciting and stunning as their religiously themed counterparts. Every culture and civilization had both a spiritual and scientific understanding of the hidden, implicate order of things and the presence of an infrastructure that was not visible to the eye—an infrastructure of realities with various connectors, triggers, and mechanisms that, when examined, sound so strikingly familiar.

The connectors in the Grid, the resonance by which we sync and create and amplify, and the field in which information passes and exchanges and transmits both require the presence of a third major connector, as well as the minor triggers and mechanisms that are at play. We cannot access other realities without three things: a vehicle to take us there, gasoline to fuel the vehicle, and the open road itself. If the open road is the Grid itself, and gasoline is the connector and trigger and mechanism, what then is the vehicle? What is the key behind all of existence itself? What unlocks the doors to other worlds, even this one we live and move and have our being in?

There is a very special connector that also acts as trigger and mechanism. In fact, it may be the whole damn enchilada itself. We cannot leave our own bodies and minds out of this equation. What is the one common denominator in any experience involving the paranormal, altered states of reality or consciousness, and anomalous events? Heck, what is the one common denominator behind the perception and experience of normal daily reality??

We are.

Meet connector number three: Us.

CHAPTER 5

REALITY IS AN INSIDE JOB

Physiology, Perception, and the Grid

There is no fixed physical reality, no single perception of the world, just numerous ways of interpreting world views as dictated by one's nervous system and the specific environment of our planetary existence.

—Deepak Chopra, "A Consciousness Based Science"

What you see is what you get!

—Geraldine, *The Flip Wilson Show*

Are you a card-carrying Democrat or a loyal Republican? Your political beliefs matter not to us, but did you know that your brain could indicate political preference? A scientific study published in the *American Journal of Political Science* in 2012 suggests that brain scans show a difference in the

77

parts of the brain most utilized by those leaning right and left. Peter Hatemi of Penn State University and Rose McDermott of Brown University reported that conservatives had more activity in the amygdala section, which is associated with the brain's threat response system, while individuals who considered themselves liberal and progressive appeared to have more activity in the insula, which acts as an internal monitor of feelings. Conservative brains seem to be more associated with fear of outside threats and liberals with emotions/feelings that lead to empathy.

While this study has been backed up by others like it, to suggest that an internal cause for beliefs and perception exists is incomplete, because our environment influences us, too. Even such things as a tendency toward gambling, addiction, crime, and violence can be discerned by specific activity in the brain; however, that presence doesn't always guarantee it will manifest in a person's actual experience. Thus, you could be born into a conservative family and still end up liberal, or vice versa, whether or not your brain was entrained for one, or your environment (parents, peers, society, media) overly influenced by one or the other. We still have some choice, do we not?

Which leads us to ask, how much of our reality is based on the brain's neurochemical activity and how much is based on our perception of external events? How much of our reality is really real at all? We looked in the last chapter at environmental influences that may affect our ability to perceive reality and other levels of the Grid. But what about what goes on inside of us?

The Fluidity of Perception

Perception is the ability to understand and experience reality based on input from the five senses. It is the reality we create based on physical awareness of environmental influences. Perception is not fixed, but rather based on illusion after illusion, memory and past experiences, beliefs and social conditioning, parental and peer pressure, and even media influences. Perception is what we think we see, feel, hear, taste, and touch *based greatly upon expectations and previous interpretations.*

In other words, perception is a dusty lens through which we view reality. At best, we can clean that lens enough to see more clearly, but most of the time we seem content to walk through life with dirty vision.

Although there is a purely physical cause for how we experience things through the five senses, as in light striking the retina of the eyes to create a visual image, or sound waves reaching our ears, so much of what we perceive is tainted by what we have learned in the past and our memories and expectations. The perceptual systems of the brain of both humans and animals are modular, with different sections responsible for different types of sensory information processing. Many of these modules interact and influence one another and create connections that add to experience. Over time, we layer interpretation over simple experiences to create an even more complex perception of reality, which ends up looking a lot like an onion, with layer upon layer of our own personal take on what is happening to us. Objective reality then becomes more subjective as it is influenced by the mind of the perceiver.

But the objective reality itself may be something completely different from what we end up with once our self-driven interpretation kicks in. Our brains are only able to perceive so much of the constant streams of information coming at our senses. So what of the information we chose to filter out, ignore, and set aside, because it would appear to have no immediate value to our survival and daily operation? That is the realm of the Grid, where information exists in the form of "unperceived realities" waiting to be discovered. Going back to the skyscraper imagery of chapter 1, it's like living in a huge skyscraper with over one thousand floors, each one rich with experience, but only being aware of twenty-seven of them. Thus, your perception of reality becomes those twenty-seven floors alone. Imagine what it would be like to cleanse the glass and experience all one thousand.

One of the most fun ways to toy with perception is with images that can be "seen" in different ways. The eye will usually automatically process an image based again upon existing cues, clues, and information, but point out to someone another way to see something and they can never go back to not seeing it that way again. The brain has been exposed to a new way of turning an image that may have been ambiguous into a very tangible interpretation, one that they can then point out to someone else. This works well with camouflage and biological mimicry, where creatures look like their environment and often blend in so well you don't see them until someone who has already perceived them points them out to you.

The brain sees what it needs to see until it has a need to see something else. There is also usually more than one physical stimulus involved in the translation of perception. In other

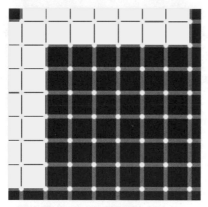

Figure 7. Stare at the white dots, and the nearby dots appear black. *Courtesy of Wikimedia*

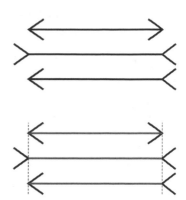

Figure 8. Though the lines look to be of different lengths, they are the same. *Courtesy of Wikimedia*

words, it might take more than just one visual cue to allow the brain to see an image, or more than just a cue from one type of sensation, say visual or auditory, to create the whole perception. Based on previous expectations and experiences, the brain even fills in incomplete images or shapes. Remember those connect-the-dot drawings in kindergarten? They were fun because they allowed our brains to naturally fill in the blanks based on what we expected the overall image to be by following the numbers in order.

WHAT CAN CAUSE MISPERCEPTIONS?

So many things can skew perception. Proximity is definitely a big one. Think of seeing something from afar and then discovering once you got closer the object was something else entirely. The brain was only able to create an interpretation with limited visual information that, when more information was available, became negated by a new perception.

This kind of misinterpretation also occurs when dealing with similar stimuli, patterns of objects, incomplete visual objects, ambiguity, and even movement, all of which make it harder for the brain to nail down exactly and consistently what it is seeing.

Another problem arises when we remember the quantum nature of particles and waves and that, at our foundation, we are not solid. Nor is anything around us. It is all vibrating, superpositioned "stuff" waiting for our act of observation or measurement to collapse its wave function and give it a fixed place in our reality. Our brains argue with us that the objects around us are solid as a rock, but our consciousness knows better. It tells us that there is more to reality than meets the eye, even if it cannot prove it.

Nothing is really real until we realize that it's real, and much of that realization is clouded by what we think and expect! Imagine standing in a forest alone. You are afraid, as there are sounds around you that you cannot identify, and you are lost. It's about to get dark. You see something off in the distance and immediately your body reacts. Fight or flight. It looks like something big—a bear? Mountain lion? Zombie? It is moving slowly toward you. You freeze, horrified. It is just . . . so . . . big . . . and misshapen in the shadows. You cannot quite make out the exact form. Is it Dick Cheney? Does he have a gun?

Alone in the woods, at dusk, your brain goes into overdrive. What is it? What should you do? Panic sets in and you turn tail and run, smacking right into a tree. Down you go, as the thing gets closer, only to turn in terror and find . . . it's a forest ranger with water, food, and a way back to your car.

Reality is just like this. We create a reality out of perceptions, interpretations, and biases, many of them mistaken, based on the available environmental cues and our own internal influences and expectations. But the thing is, *that is not reality.* As you waited in terror for the zombie-lion-bear thing to jump on you, all around you there may have been angels, demons, aliens, invisible creatures, wormholes leading to parallel worlds—escape routes into other levels of the Grid you did not see because your internal influences were so focused on the available environmental cues.

This does not mean those realities do not exist. You just didn't expect them to, and therefore did not experience them. Good thing, too, because in one of those realities, it really could have been a bear-lion-zombie attack.

In the various levels of the Grid, there are realities we cannot normally experience and do not normally perceive. But each and every day we get glimpses of these other realities, even experiences of them. And yet some individuals do not. Why is this? If we all have the same shared reality in which we agree that blue is blue and a chair is a chair and Christmas falls on December 25 each year, and if we are all made the same physically with blood and guts and bone and brain, why is it that one person can experience or perceive something completely differently from another?

Reality may be more of an inside job than we think.

THE INTERNAL CONNECTION

The human body is a strange brew of chemical and biological interactions, all designed to give us the experience of being alive. From blood type to body build to bone density, genetic makeup, brain chemical levels, and hormones, we are machines that may look similar outside and inside, and yet are tweaked to allow for some degree of individuality. When all of these interactions run smoothly, we feel good and are healthy and operate at a maximum. But when these interactions are not functioning as they should, disease and disorder enter the picture. Our concern is this: Can these physical interactions in the body have anything to do with the experience of other realities?

It's hard to imagine that your blood type or the amount of cortisol or serotonin in your body has a direct influence on your ability to perceive the unperceivable, but there is ample circumstantial evidence to show that they do. We say circumstantial because we cannot prove it in an empirical sense—at least, not yet—although studies like the one we mentioned at the start of this chapter certainly are intriguing. But science is getting ever closer to showing that internal and external work together to create this reality, and enough people have experienced other realities when just the right alignment of inner/outer is achieved.

Did you know that your brain contains a trace amount of a chemical that could make you believe you are seeing a ghost (as well as experience or perceive a whole litany of other paranormal phenomena)? DMT (dimethyltryptamine) is a psychoactive compound and is considered a psychedelic drug because it can cause out-of-body experiences (OBEs), hallucinations, the sense of the presence of spirit or alien life-forms, as well as divine visions, precognition, and déjà vu. DMT is also a naturally occurring trace amino neurotransmitter/neuromodulator in the brain, derived from the essential amino acid tryptophan and structurally similar to serotonin, melatonin, and the psychedelic tryptamines, such as 5-MeO-DMT, bufotenin, psilocin, and psilocybin. DMT is present in the brain's pineal gland in tiny amounts, yet because of its ability to produce wild and wacky experiences of other levels of reality in larger doses, it is classified as an illegal drug. It is also an active ingredient in ayahuasca, the sacred brew used by shamans and indigenous peoples in the Amazon and elsewhere to induce the experience of alternate realities and access the inner eye.

Between 1990 and 1995, Dr. Rick Strassman became the first scientist to ever conduct government-approved research experiments on human beings using psychedelics and hallucinogenic substances, focusing on DMT. At the time he was a tenured associate professor of psychiatry at the University of New Mexico's School of Medicine in Albuquerque. Strassman's theory was that DMT would be released from the pineal gland in larger amounts when a person was on the verge of dreaming or dying, and DMT might account for the visions experienced during NDEs. He chose DMT because it is an endogenous psychedelic found in hundreds of species of plants and mammals, including humans. Because of his years of interest in Eastern religions and brain physiology, he saw the potential for DMT to mediate spiritual experiences and psychedelic drug states similar to the effects of meditation.

Strassman utilized more than sixty volunteers who received what he calls "the God or Spirit molecule" in doses large enough to cause some type of vision or sense of presence, many of which involved encounters with entities that could be described as alien. Some volunteers reported seeing strange geometric shapes and patterns that they could change at will.

These experiences are all documented in Strassman's book *DMT: The Spirit Molecule* and suggest that this substance we all have in our brains has the ability to transform our experience of reality in just the right dose.

Strassman also experimented with psilocybin, which is a naturally occurring alkaloid found in certain types of hallucinogenic mushrooms. His research opened new doors to the nature of consciousness and the ability to alter consciousness to literally transcend normal waking state experiences. Strassman's research continues through his colleagues Dr. Steven A. Barker and Andrew C. Stone at the Cottonwood Research Foundation.

Strassman's findings with DMT mirror those of Graham Hancock utilizing ayahuasca in his book *Supernatural,* which documents common imagery and experiences on hallucinogenic substances. The Brazilian government made DMT a legal supplement after studying it for years, including its usage in the shaman's brew. Much of this imagery is archetypal in quality and suggests a collective unconscious at work that transcends any geographic, religious, or traditional boundaries. These images and concepts are experienced by a variety of people from a variety of cultures; they know no bias of race or gender or belief. Other types of drugs, both naturally occurring and chemically created, do the same, creating everything from mild states of euphoria to full-on trips of the mind down the rabbit hole.

Because DMT occurs in the human brain, is it possible that our experiences of the Grid, and what we might deem paranormal or anomalous events, happen in a natural setting when some external influence acts upon us that causes an increase of DMT to be released?

There are many studies involving the role of neurochemicals and paranormal experiences. Besides DMT, tryptamines, ketamine, and B-carboline alkaloids have been linked to psi experiences such as OBEs, NDEs, even ESP, telepathy, clairvoyance, and precognition. Some of these studies are outlined in *Advances in Parapsychological Research,* published by the Parapsychology Foundation, including more than 200 scientific papers written solely on the subject of psychoactive drugs and paranormal experiences.

The use of both clinical and recreational drugs such as ketamine, a substance commonly used for anesthesia of animals and often referred to as Special K, certainly plays a role. Ketamine is known to cause intense experiences of being out of the body and other very powerful sensations of spatial distortion.

As these and other studies point out, the drugs in question offer similar experiences such as OBEs and psychic ability, with an occasional rarity such as telekinetic ability, but for those who are not on any kind of drug, these experiences can be triggered by the brain and body chemicals themselves, if in just the right amounts. An altered state of perception, mind, and reality can easily occur based on the ingestion of a substance that sends our brain's neurotransmitters into overdrive, or that disrupts the natural chemical balance to create a different state of being, including varied perceptions of time, space, and our place in the fabric of reality. It is common for ayahuasca to cause distortions in the perception of time, either slowing it down or speeding it up, or creating a sense of complete and utter timelessness, as if we have for the time being (pun intended) escaped the confines of linear past, present, and future and entered a realm where all exist at once.

Zero-point field. Akasha. Kingdom of Heaven. The Grid.

We don't necessarily need to be "on" anything to make these experiences happen, although many of the substances that we deem "drugs" are natural and were probably ingested as a part of the daily lives of those who lived off the land, and still do. To these people, anomalous and paranormal experiences are part of their reality, because they are part of the world they naturally exist in. For those of us living in cities and buildings and out of touch with nature, paranormal experiences are something to be feared or approached with caution.

Fear itself was also found to be an influence on whether or not someone taking a particular drug would experience the paranormal, suggesting that emotions play a role in the release of certain brain chemicals, and ramping up or suppressing certain brain activity. The power of the brain goes beyond just chemical interactions. Our emotions, beliefs, and perceptions are already at work influencing what we will experience and what we will block out or filter—especially if an experience was traumatic.

When we experience something out of the ordinary without the aid of drugs, we tend to view these experiences as abnormalities, although they can happen for perfectly explainable reasons that include both environmental and internal causes, and vary from person to person according to the amounts present of key chemicals and hormones, including serotonin, DMT, cortisol, and many others. Though the scientific literature may indicate that psychedelic drugs can cause these experiences to happen more often, and even increase the number of experiences one will have as one continues to do the drug, taking hallucinogens like DMT or mushrooms is not entirely necessary. Our own bodies seem to possess an inherent ability to take a walk now and then through the Grid. In other words, we don't need to eat a mushroom or smoke or snort something to trip a little.

So let's remove the entire drug aspect, legal and illegal, natural and manmade, from the picture for a minute, and focus on a more natural "drug" that has many of the same effects.

NATURAL CHEMICAL CONNECTIONS

DMT has a molecular structure similar to both melatonin and serotonin.

Serotonin, also known as 5-hydroxytryptamine, is a hormone found in the pineal gland, the digestive tract (gut), the central nervous system, and blood platelets, and it is one of the body's chief hormones that regulates certain cell and organ activity. It is also a neurotransmitter, meaning it sends nerve impulses across the space between neurons, or nerve cells, which are called synapses. Serotonin plays an important part in the regulation of learning, sleep, and vasoconstriction (the narrowing of blood vessel walls as cells move through the veins). Altered levels of serotonin in the brain can cause depression and anxiety, but also calmness, contentment, and a sense of well-being. It can also affect how much you sleep, as well as dream activity and intensity.

What most people don't know is that about 90 percent of the body's serotonin is found not in the brain, but in the gut, in the enterochromaffin cells, which regulate intestinal movements and trigger digestion. Thus, the gut feelings some people claim to get may be the effects of serotonin in the gut itself, working via the central nervous system to send signals to the brain that something is amiss or needs our attention.

In a May 2009 issue of *Scientific American* a study conducted at the University of Essex in England found that people with the long versions of the gene for the serotonin transporter protein, which controls serotonin levels in brain cells, paid more attention to positive imagery than negative imagery, all but ignoring the negative. The opposite results were found for those who carried the shorter gene. The study, involving ninety-seven patients, suggested that depending on their serotonin levels, people were more positive or negative in their outlook on life, more glass half-full or glass half-empty. Thus, the presence or lack of certain levels of this particular neurotransmitter had a definite impact on what a person chose to perceive, and what they chose to ignore or set aside.

Of the primary neurotransmitters, the other two being dopamine and norepinephrine, serotonin influences our moods and perceptions, as it also is involved in the regulations of emotion, memory, and learning in a way that affects our perception of reality and our approach to it. Lower levels of serotonin have even been linked anecdotally to being more open to belief in the paranormal and religion, with higher levels more often associated with objective, empirical views of spirituality and religion.

There are other important chemicals in the brain and body that may influence how we experience reality. Melatonin also shares a structure similar to DMT and mescaline and is notorious for promoting not just good sleep, but intense and freaky dreams! Secreted by the pineal gland, melatonin is the hormone that regulates the sleep and waking cycle and the body's circadian rhythm. The body produces more melatonin when it is dark, and less when exposed to light, and disruptions in the cycle can result in insomnia, jet lag, and even poor vision ability during the day.

Because of its similar properties to DMT, melatonin can produce incredibly vivid and intense dreams. Peak production of natural melatonin in the body is between 1:00 a.m. and 3:00 a.m., which interestingly corresponds to anecdotal paranormal activity increases. Is it because melatonin, either not enough or too much of it, is influencing something in the brain that perceives what is not visually there? Melatonin plays a key role in regulating the female menstrual cycle, including initiating menopause. Might this account for why women seem more intuitive, psychic, and even more prone to reporting visions of ghosts or spirits? The lack of sleep may be just as much of an issue as too much melatonin in the body. More on this in the next chapter.

Hormones and brain chemicals have a distinct role in how we function, and how well we function, both physically and psychologically. Imbalances of naturally occurring chemicals disrupt our ability to operate in a normal way in our waking world, and in extreme cases may cause us to lose touch with reality altogether. Have you ever been sleep deprived? Both visual and auditory hallucinations are common when someone lacks proper sleep, something people who suffer from PTSD can attest to. Even being deeply depressed or in a state of paranoid anxiety can create a reality that does not entirely exist in an objective sense. Our bodies, and our brains, trip us up. This is never clearer than when we fall in love.

The very biological act that is designed to keep the human race thriving causes a rush of chemicals to flood the brain. The combination of particular neurotransmitters causes us to feel a sense of euphoria when love strikes, and yet the sensation of our boundaries being lowered and the openness and joy we feel being in love is really the result of perfectly natural machinations. We say love is elusive, wondrous, and even inexplicable and indescribable, and yet . . . we all believe love is a real thing, do we not?

When love happens, the sex hormones testosterone and estrogen drive the action. Lust and attraction are powered by three main neurotransmitters—adrenaline, dopamine, and serotonin, all of which have their role in getting us hooked on someone. Remember, these are biological urges with a foundation of neurochemical interactions, all designed to create babies.

Once the attachment stage kicks in, the "cuddle hormone" oxytocin is released, mainly during orgasm, believe it or not, but this deepens the bond between two people needed to go the distance in a relationship long enough to result in a baby. Oxytocin helps mothers bond with babies and helps the release of breast milk at the sound of a crying baby, hungry for sustenance. Vasopressin, another hormone, also may be involved in creating a desire for long-term bonding.

In a study conducted at the University of Pisa, Italy, Dr. Donatella Marazziti followed twenty couples who claimed to be madly in love for less than six months and found that the same brain mechanisms occurred in the brains of the wildly and obsessively beloved that occur in the brains of people with obsessive-compulsive disorder. Low serotonin levels were to blame for both, proving that when people fall in love, it literally changes their thought processes, patterns, and behaviors. It also blinds us to our lover's faults and problems, thus the saying "love is blind."

Love changes our entire perception of reality.

Phenylethylamine, or PEA, is also a suspect in the mysteries of the emotions that lead to love. This central nervous system stimulant is found in the brain and assists in arousal of emotion. Think about the meaning of the phrase "pea brain." Some studies in the past linked chocolate intake to a rise in levels of PEA, thus creating the feeling of being in love while eating a candy bar, but these results have since been negated. The body absorbs very little PEA from chocolate, although there certainly are other foods that act as aphrodisiacs. This does not explain, though, why so many people fall in love with chocolate!

Food and drink also affect our moods, our bodies, and our minds, because, in turn, they influence the levels of all of these chemicals that already exist in the brain. We are, it seems, unknowingly controlled by our own bodily functions, at least to the degree that we allow it. Although try *not* falling in love with someone you are falling for to see how powerful these neurochemical cocktails can be.

So even this mystery of love is really not much of a mystery at all.

We live in a stress-filled world, one where we are surrounded by fast food and polluted water, air, and soil. In an effort to keep up, our natural levels of many of these chemicals have been altered significantly. Cortisol and adrenaline, the fight or flight stress hormones, are surging and staying at high levels when they should be balanced, thus resulting in more and more stress-related illness and disease. Dopamine, which keeps us happy and satisfied, may be in short supply, which results in cranky dispositions and miserable personalities. We are an anxious, depressed species, overworked and overwhelmed, and it is not just affecting our inner physiology, but our outer world as well.

Because our perception of reality is directly influenced by these biochemical functions, we see threats where we did not see them before, and we envision problems that may or may not exist. The sheer volume of information our brains must process, thanks to the progress of technology and the presence of electronic intrusion into every aspect of our lives (are you reading this on your cell phone or tablet?), is overwhelming as we filter out what we don't need in order to preserve what we do.

Imagine the information we are filtering out right now at this point in history. Maybe it's the entire Grid itself. When we are most stressed, we feel the most disconnected—not just from ourselves, but also from any sense of a greater whole that we may exist in. The feelings of being connected and at one with the world around us slip away, leaving us with a powerful sense of separation that we are convinced is our real reality. And yet, those experiences continue to happen to us that poke and prod us to reconsider our notion of what reality really is. Problem is, we have to be paying attention to notice our misperception of separateness in the first place.

Most of the other realities we propose are in the Grid may be presenting themselves to us all the time. But we tune them out, willingly or unwillingly, in our attempt to just survive. Our bodies may hold incredible keys and clues to the doors to altered realities and states of perception that allow us to move between them. Too bad our ability to open those doors has been so compromised.

Our bodies are intricately designed to keep us alive and living the life that is before us, at least to the best of our ability, and that is the most critical aspect of being a human. Every part of our physicality is meant to keep us grounded in reality, at least *this reality,* so that we can grow up and become an adult and hold down a job, pay exorbitant taxes, raise a family, and do our part to contribute to society. Our chemicals and hormones, our blood, our organs and cells, minds and brains all are given a particular role in the perception, manifestation, and experience of this reality. When they work together well, we thrive. We might even find love and happiness and purpose. When they are imbalanced or influenced by outside cues, we suffer, become ill, or experience an altered sense of reality.

But our physiology can also open the doors to other realities. What doesn't kill us makes us stronger, and what we don't pay attention to may be the truth about just how much more there is to this thing called life than meets the eye.

CHAPTER 6

GHOSTS IN THE GRID

Paranormal Realities

Reality is merely an illusion, albeit a very persistent one.
—ALBERT EINSTEIN

It is wonderful that five thousand years have now elapsed since the creation of the world, and still it is undecided whether or not there has ever been an instance of the spirit of any person appearing after death. All argument is against it; but all belief is for it.
—SAMUEL JOHNSON

As of March 2013, a Google search for the word "paranormal" shows more than 114 million hits. Obviously, a lot of folks are interested in the topic! The term "paranormal" was coined in the early nineteenth century and generally denotes experiences that according to thefreedictionary.com are "beyond the range of normal experience or scientific explanation."

While some may automatically associate the word paranormal with ghost hunting, the field of paranormal research actually encompasses a far broader spectrum of subjects. Topics such as extraterrestrial encounters, cryptozoology (the study of animals which have not been scientifically categorized), OOPArt (out-of-place artifacts), parapsychology (experimental investigation of the paranormal), ESP, astrology, reincarnation, channeling, and psionics all fall under the purview of "paranormal" due to the fact that they are all currently beyond the range of normal experience or scientific explanation. Because of its popularity, however, we'll start our discussion of the paranormal with ghosts.

Flip through the channels on TV, and it is very likely that you will run across at least one paranormal show. Shows like *Ghost Hunters, Destination Truth, Paranormal Cops, Ghost Adventures, Paranormal State,* and a handful of others seem to currently be all the rage. In fact, the glut of paranormal programming has spawned countless hobbyist paranormal researchers to form grassroots organizations chartered to investigate paranormal and anomalous phenomena. With no formal training, certification, or peer-review process, these enthusiastic folks (oftentimes under the mistaken pretext of following strict scientific methodology) seek out and investigate reportedly haunted locations throughout the world.

In their zealous quest for discovery, what exactly are they investigating? Demons? Ghosts? Spirits of the deceased? Their own internalized psychological issues? If you have ever watched any of the aforementioned paranormal shows, or even participated in a paranormal investigation, then you likely already know that there isn't 100 percent infallible proof. There is no photographic evidence, no "smoking gun." No audio proof of life beyond the grave. There is certainly an overwhelming amount of anecdotal evidence, but nothing substantiated or provable.

So, does this mean that upon death we simply "wink out" of existence, like a light switch being turned off? Is it truly "ashes to ashes, dust to dust"? We know that everyone and everything will eventually die. It is an inescapable fact.

It is a curious thing, the death of a loved one. We all know that our time in this world is limited, and that eventually all of us will end up underneath some sheet, never to wake up. And yet it is always a surprise when it happens to someone we know. It is like walking up the stairs to your bedroom in the dark, and thinking there is one more stair than there is. Your foot falls down, through the air, and there is a sickly moment of dark surprise as you try and readjust the way you thought of things.

—LEMONY SNICKET, HORSERADISH: BITTER TRUTHS YOU CAN'T AVOID

Let's go back to our ghost-hunter friends for a moment. What if these amateur researchers are actually investigating phenomena as real and alive as you and I? What if upon physical death we somehow transfer to another medium, a different realm? Suppose death truly is *not* the end, but merely the beginning.

Is Death Final?

Let's change gears for a moment and discuss two personal experiences that coauthor Larry recently experienced.

Last year, I lost both of my parents within four months of each other. They met during German class in high school where my mom tutored my dad. They fell in love and spent the next forty-nine years together, absolutely inseparable. Their relationship was incredible—they were truly soul mates, and words cannot describe the depth of love that they felt for each other.

My father contracted an extremely rare brain disease four years ago, and through it all my mom was by his side. After a long, valiant fight, my dad passed away in March 2012, and as often happens when a spouse passes away, my mom followed suit in August.

For as long as I can remember, my mother harbored an intense thirst for all things paranormal. In fact, anything mysterious or unexplained seemed to always be a topic of discussion for us. On multiple occasions we discussed if there was any way we might attempt contact from the other side to let the other person who was left behind know that we were OK. A few months after my father passed away, my mom told me she had a visit from my dad, and they discussed the first thing that they wanted to do when they were reunited with each other. According to my mom, they decided they wanted to visit all the places they had lived together.

I didn't think too much about that conversation until the day after my mom passed away. I was sitting in my office when I received a telephone call from the alarm company that monitors the alarm in my folks' house. According to the representative, the motion sensors in their home were tracking movement from the kitchen to the living room. As they dispatched the police, the lady told me that they were seeing continued movement between those two rooms. Since there had not been one single false alarm in the twenty-three years my parents had lived there, my first thought was that some miscreant had realized that the house was now a prime target and had broken in, hopeful that they could have carte blanche.

I quickly called my brother Jon, and we both raced to the house. Jon and I arrived at the same time as the police. As we unlocked the front door, the three of us checked and cleared each room . . . nothing. No broken windows, no signs of forced entry, nothing disturbed or removed. After the police left, Jon and I sat on the floor in the living room, staring at the motion detector mounted close to the ceiling. We tried to figure out what could have caused such an unusual, extended false alarm; however, we couldn't come up with any rational explanation. Then it hit me like a ton of bricks: the conversation with my mother.

My parents had come back to the last place they lived together to visit, and setting the alarm off was either an accident or perhaps a way to prove to me, the analytical, skeptical one, that they were together.

As an interesting side note, shortly after my dad got sick, we converted the living room into living quarters for both of them. They spent the last three and a half years living in that room, and never traveled upstairs or throughout the rest of the house—only to the kitchen and living room.

The alarm was reset and has yet to trigger again.

○ ◎ ○

On the same evening the alarm incident occurred, I got into bed at my usual time (around 9:30 p.m.) and tossed and turned for a while until finally falling asleep from exhaustion. I was awakened at 3:23 a.m. by my cell phone ringing. When I looked at the caller ID it said "Blocked." Ninety-nine percent of the time when I received a blocked call it was my mother, as she still used an old analog cell phone that did not transmit caller ID information.

When I answered the phone I could hear a tremendous amount of static and a voice that sounded far off in the distance. Instinctually, I said "Mom? Is that you?" I was not able to discern exactly what was being said, but it definitely sounded like an older female voice mixed in with the static. The call lasted exactly thirty-four seconds before it disconnected. As I lay there trying to process what had just happened the phone rang again. Again, this "Blocked" call seemed to be comprised of all static with a voice far off in the distance. I repeated, "Mom, can you hear me?" Static. Twenty-three seconds later the call terminated and has never reoccurred. Interestingly, we later found out that my mom first began experiencing signs of respiratory distress at approximately 3:23 a.m.—the same time that I received the mysterious phone call.

The next morning I began researching possible explanations for my weird phone call and quickly discovered that I am not alone. Apparently, this type of experience is more common than I would have guessed. What I discovered is that "calls from beyond" usually occur within twenty-four hours after the caller's death.

There are a number of reports on paranormal forums and websites about people receiving calls from dead loved ones. Often the person receiving the call was particularly close to the deceased, but when they would ask the caller what life was like on the "other side," the caller would hang up. Calls like this could go on for a while and then just stop without rhyme or reason.

Were these experiences proof of life beyond the grave? To answer that question, perhaps we need to redefine not only our understanding of the cyclical nature of life but also the verbiage we use to define and describe it. Words like "deceased," "dying," and "died" all confer an ultimate finality that may not necessarily be the true indicator of reality.

ARPAST AND THE ENVIRONMENT

Coauthor Larry runs the Arkansas Paranormal and Anomalous Studies Team (ARPAST), one of the country's largest and most respected paranormal research organizations. Coauthor Marie is the director of special projects, and we have together been intrigued by how much of the paranormal might actually be evidence of other levels of reality, and how much of it is a result of specific external and internal triggers and mechanisms.

Since it is impossible to predict when an anomalous event will occur, ARPAST has chosen to focus primarily on studying the only physically quantifiable element—environmental effects. For something to interact within our physicality, it has to follow our known physical laws of nature. Using scientific methodologies, state-of-the-art equipment, and custom software, ARPAST has been able to rule out any possible explanatory causes for paranormal phenomena.

Over the course of six years of field research, ARPAST has pioneered a number of theories and concepts regarding the connection between environmental conditions and paranormal phenomena:

- ◎ We found that "ghosts" compromise a wide array of phenomena that appear to arise from a number of different causes.

- ◎ We discovered that reportedly "haunted" locations tend to be extremely rich in Jungian archetypal symbology, thus demonstrating that these places are far more about living human consciousness than dead people.

- ◎ We verified on numerous occasions what seemed to be low but still measurable magnetic anomalies (>20 percent of geomagnetic ambient, or ~.1 gauss) in locations that had reported unusual activity.

- ◎ We detected extremely low frequency (ELF) spikes in the infrasonic range (less than 20 Hz) in locations reporting either unusual or paranormal phenomena.

- ◎ We noted the presence of localized thermal inversions of more than 5 degrees Fahrenheit in areas correlating to recent unusual activity.

- ◎ On numerous occasions, we identified a slight but still measurable (more than .02 inches of mercury) barometric pressure drops in rooms where unusual activity had been recently reported.

- ◎ We discovered occasional atmospheric ion count changes and EM field distortions in areas correlating to unusual activity.

- ◎ Immediately before a "Class A" EVP (electronic voice phenomena) capture, we identified an impulse "pop" of approx. .5-1 dB(A) above ambient. This phenomenon seems to be universal, and Larry was interviewed about this occurrence on the Discovery Channel's popular show *Ghost Lab* (2009, Season 1, Episode 10).

Beyond the environmental factors, we discovered something far more important. We discovered that the *experiencer* is the most important factor in every single report of paranormal activity. You and I are innate parts of the equation, as are our physiology, our bodies, and our brains. As we discussed in previous chapters, the external environmental influences and our internal physiology may need to be specifically aligned to create the potential for paranormal phenomena to manifest.

If the exterior and interior resonance is off, no experience of alternate realities or other worlds, including the phenomena and entities they may contain, occurs. Most of the time we cannot control the alignment of these influences, as we are still struggling to understand exactly what needs to be aligned! But this may explain the erratic nature of paranormal phenomena. It just doesn't occur at will; the recipe has to be exact for the outcome to manifest.

In ARPAST, experiments were also conducted where members and visitors attending a paranormal investigation were fed false stories about the location's history and who may have died there. Not surprisingly, at least 75 percent of the time almost everyone attending would have an experience mirror at least one, if not more, of the false stories told to them before the ghost hunt began. This proves that most of the events reported were tainted with the bias of previous knowledge, expectation, and just plain wanting to conform and be a part of something exciting. Indeed, these are real and valid reasons for why people sometimes believe they've experienced something out of the ordinary. But it doesn't make their experience true.

Does this mean that these people simply made it all up or imagined it? Not necessarily. It could mean that they actually had a part in the manifestation and perception of the events, especially in the cases where more than one person experienced false information at the same time. Contagious thought works like a virus, infecting the minds of the collective as it does individuals. ARPAST repeatedly found that you can plant a story and have aspects of that story—physical aspects, such as voices and sounds and even spectral and shadowy figures—seemingly manifest as real events. People can be touched, scratched, feel heat or extreme cold, and see and hear things that may or may not really be there but were told would be.

Whether all of this comes from the minds of the experiencers, or it is a combination of collective belief and some external force that allows for an opening to exist where there was none before, people are having real experiences that often leave physical traces and marks, as well as emotional ones.

We are convinced that much of what we call the paranormal is really normal manifestations of other levels of the Grid. Whether it is a ghost, a shadow person, a UFO, or a cryptid, we may be dealing with things that, in their neck of the woods, are the normal ones, and we the paranormal. Those with the right physiological brew of hormones and brain chemicals and blood types may be just at the right place at the right time, when the air is in a specific temperature range, the barometric pressure is just right, there is a specific ion count, and EM fluctuates in just the right direction to get a peek behind the curtain.

THE POLTERGEIST ENIGMA

One of the best examples of the alignment of external and internal triggers and mechanisms in the paranormal is the poltergeist. Known as "noisy ghosts" from the German etymology, *poltern* meaning "to make sound" and *geist* meaning "ghost," a poltergeist really isn't a ghost at all, but instead more of a manifestation of both external and internal influences that actually can move objects and create havoc. Because of its negative and even terrifying quality, many people associate poltergeist activity with demons, but some of the more serious scientific inquiry into the phenomenon suggests something different.

Parapsychologist Nandor Fodor speculated that the cause of poltergeist activity was linked directly to a human agent, usually a child or teenager, and that the activity had nothing to do with entities at all, let alone demons. Fodor, a psychologist and author of *On the Trail of the Poltergeist* and *Story of the Poltergeist Down the Centuries,* proposed that poltergeist activity was a manifestation of conflicts occurring with the subconscious that were able to take on physical form.

William G. Roll, another noted psychologist, studied well over a hundred different poltergeist cases and posited that the agents were often children or teenagers experiencing recurrent neuronal discharges, resulting in epileptic symptoms that could be behind the "recurrent spontaneous psychokinesis" (RSPK). These discharges from the brain actually could affect the human agent's surroundings in the form of moving objects and things levitating or flying across the room. It was a perfect brew of the brain and the environment working in tandem to create a paranormal phenomenon we still don't quite understand.

Roll, who recently passed away, was a very respected parapsychologist associated with the Parapsychology Laboratory of Duke University for a number of years. He even coined the term RSPK in a research paper that documented his very first case of poltergeist activity, which involved a twelve-year-old boy. As Roll's work progressed, he looked at geomagnetic perturbations, seismic activity, weather, radiation, and even quantum mechanics to pinpoint the cause of this strange phenomenon. His final research presented his case for a combination of quantum physics and neuroscience that linked poltergeists to psi fields present around every object and living thing. These energy fields are made up of nonphysical subatomic particles such as psitrons and psychons that contain psi information that Roll and others like him alleged could be the carriers of ESP, remote viewing, psychic phenomena, clairvoyance, precognition, and even ghosts. This field could exist both in the mind and outside of the body, and information would move between the brain and physical objects to cause them to manifest as poltergeist activity.

Roll authored a number of books and papers for parapsychology journals, and his last book was released in 2004, *Unleashed: Of Poltergeists and Murder: The Curious Story of Tina Resch*. His work carried the poltergeist phenomenon well away from the usual ghost labels and into a field that blended the mysteries of the human brain with those of the paranormal.

Like the akashic field of Ervin Laszlo or the zero-point field of quantum theory, this psi field is a grid of connectivity that opens a door for interactions between the internal neurological actions of the brain and the external environment. This field is invisible and operates at the quantum level, and though we may not see where the cause takes place, we see the wide variety of effects that emerge from the field as all sorts of explainable and unexplainable phenomena. We can all access and use this field, although maybe not by will or voluntarily, which might even be attributed to the manifestation of apparitions, ghosts, and other entities that appear to some people and not to others. It isn't that some people don't see them because they don't believe in such phenomena, but rather they don't perceive them because their own psi field may not be aligned with the external psi field in a way that allows for it.

How can two people stand next to each other and not see the same thing? How can a group of thirteen attend a ghost hunt and only three people have any kind of anomalous experiences? How can one person bend spoons with his mind and another not be able to move a feather? These inconsistencies again point more to differences in physiology than one person being overly imaginative, a fraud, or a charlatan, although they certainly exist in the paranormal as they do in any other field. But millions of people all over the world see ghosts, experience psychic phenomena, see UFOs and even alien occupants, come face-to-face with a bizarre creature that appears out of nowhere, and glimpse alternate realities during such events as time slips and near-death experiences, all of which occur on one or more levels of the Grid.

A ghost, therefore, may be a living being somewhere else, or perhaps an imprint of information on the psi field, energy that takes on form and physical appearance for the eyes of those able to perceive. Just the same, a ghost may also be a loved one you know and recognize who has passed on, but passed on to where? Another level of the Grid.

We cannot research the unknown from only one perspective or point of view; nor can we assume that anomalous phenomena come only from here and abide only by our laws of nature and physics, and therefore obey those same laws. The paranormal cannot be identified and explained with tools and equipment designed only to measure environmental effects in this one reality. But what if the supernatural is all in the mind or the wild imagination of those who believe in it? This is a narrow-minded assumption and a tunnel vision of understanding that will never give us the answers we seek.

The sheer volume of experiences and research into those experiences shows that we may be dealing with more than one reality, with laws and causes and effects our own scientific method falls short of dissecting, duplicating, and debunking.

In the Grid, anything and everything exists—even a dead zone.

CHAPTER 7

LIFE AND DEATH IN THE GRID

Men fear Death as children fear to go in the dark; and as that natural fear in children is increased with tales, so is the other.

—FRANCIS BACON, "OF DEATH"

According to current medical understanding of the brain and mind, there is no way I could have experienced even a dim and limited consciousness during my time in the coma, much less the hyper-vivid and completely coherent odyssey I underwent.

—DR. EBEN ALEXANDER, *NEWSWEEK*, OCT. 9, 2012

If the Grid is real, then could death simply be traveling to another level?

Have you heard the remarkable story of James Leininger? James was a two-year-old boy living a normal life in Lafayette,

Louisiana. James was like most kids his age—carefree and playful. Except that over the course of the next four years, he recalled detailed memories of a past lifetime as an American fighter pilot who died in combat over Iwo Jima during World War II. Incredibly, James had innate and intimate knowledge of World War II–specific airplanes, as well as recall of historical details and facts far beyond what any six-year-old could possibly have.

Thousands of such stories exist, many documented in books and on TV shows, of children who are able to remember events, people, and places that existed in a time before they were ever born. Are these children time travelers, or are they actually recalling, perhaps on a cellular level, memories of their past?

RECALLING A PAST LIFE

Reincarnation research is considered a branch of parapsychology and is generally shunned by mainstream science. But serious researchers such as psychiatrists Ian Stevenson and Jim B. Tucker have examined more than 2,500 case studies of children who claim to remember a past life. Stevenson, from the University of Virginia School of Medicine, worked over forty years to document such cases and wrote a number of books about his findings, including *Where Reincarnation and Biology Intersect*. Stevenson's work was then taken up by psychiatrist Jim B. Tucker, who wrote *Life before Life* when Stevenson retired. They also published many peer-reviewed papers about their findings with children between the ages of three and seven all over the world who seemed to be able to recall stunning details about past lives in terms of locations, deceased people, and specific events. Often the children would even remember how they died, usually violently or traumatically. Stevenson also examined birthmarks and birth defects that he claimed, in approximately 35 percent of the cases, matched the manner of injuries or illnesses that led to the death of the person each child claimed to have been in the past.

After the age of seven, such memories seem to dissipate, which interestingly corresponds to a shift from the delta brain waves of infancy to the more sophisticated theta and alpha brain waves children operate in up until age twelve. Between the ages of two and six, theta brain waves develop and increase. These brain waves are associated with imagination and creativity. At this time alpha waves are also becoming more prominent, which are receptive, passive, and relaxed yet alert, also conducive to daydreams and a light hypnotic state. Then, around age twelve, children begin to operate primarily in the "wake state" of beta waves, and perhaps once the child's brain matures to this more functional state, the connective links to the past begin to vanish as new memories and experiences are imprinted upon the gray matter. Now one could say that this early stage is proof of the power of a good imagination, but we all know that even a good imagination cannot create factual, provable details that a child would have no access to. Maybe the brain wave differences over age discern who can better walk which levels of the Grid . . . and who cannot (see chapter 5!).

Other scientific researchers have studied the same phenomena, refusing to just pass off these childhood memories as overactive imaginations and anomalies of memory areas of the brain. No, these children were recalling things they could never have seen or experienced, and at a time in their lives when even fantasy and attention seeking and suggestibility could not cause such amazing detail.

We know that the brain does not survive death, so how could a child recall memories of a time before he was born? Perhaps the early brain has access to the field of all information that we call the Grid. And perhaps the concept of death as finality is not at all what death *really is*. We believe that death is more of a transition, not an ending, like turning the pages of a book from one page to the next.

ONE DOCTOR'S EXPERIENCE

In 2008, Harvard neurosurgeon Eben Alexander contracted an extremely rare form of bacterial meningitis that quickly spread to his neocortex, the area of the brain that primarily handles sensory perception and conscious thought. For seven days, Alexander lay in a deep coma. For all intents and purposes, Alexander remained "brain dead" throughout this period. But that is only how it appeared on the surface. During the course of the coma, Alexander describes how he "journeyed to another, larger dimension of the universe, a dimension I'd never dreamed existed." There he found "big, puffy, pink-white" clouds against a "deep, black-blue sky" and "flocks of transparent, shimmering beings . . . quite simply different from anything I have known on this planet."

Alexander has extremely vivid recall of the entire experience and remembers meeting a young woman with high cheekbones, deep-blue eyes, and "golden brown tresses" who, along with "millions" of butterflies, spoke to him telepathically . . . seemingly "without using any words."

"You are loved and cherished, dearly, forever," she told the doctor. "You have nothing to fear. There is nothing you can do wrong." Alexander recounts his story in graphic and vivid detail, despite the fact that the portions of his brain responsible for visual imagery, cognitive thought, and memory were effectively shut down.

Did Eban Alexander visit heaven, or was he walking another part of the Grid, as real and alive as he was on the level he left behind, even if only temporarily?

Near-death experiences are often passed off as neurological anomalies, but more and more neurologists and scientists are wondering why they are so hard to explain and brush away as simply existing within the confines of normal brain activity. Take the case of Atlanta singer-songwriter Pam Reynolds, whose story has been documented by the BCC and Mario Beauregard in his book *Brain Wars: The Scientific Battle over the Existence of the Mind and the Proof That Will Change the Way We Live Our Lives*. An associate research professor at the Departments of Psychology and Radiology and the Neuroscience Research Center at the University of Montreal, Beauregard examines Reynolds's experience after she suffered from a dangerous aneurysm close to her brain stem. It was deemed too dangerous to do even standard surgery, but if the aneurysm burst, she would die. So she opted for a daring surgical procedure called Operation Standstill offered by neurosurgeon Dr. Robert Spetzler in Phoenix, Arizona.

The procedure would bring Reynolds's body temperature down to a point where she was essentially dead so that her brain would not function, but would survive. The extremely low temperature would allow the swollen blood vessels to soften up and then be operated on with less risk of them bursting. Once complete, the surgical team would return her body to a normal temperature, hopefully before any damage could be done.

During the process, she had what is now considered one of the most famous out-of-body experiences ever to be corroborated by other witnesses. As a team of about twenty doctors, nurses, and technicians conducted the operation on Reynolds, even taping her eyes shut and securing her ears with gauze and tape, Speltzer began to cut through her brain with a surgical saw. As things progressed, despite having no sense of sight or hearing, Reynolds was later able to describe her observations, including how they had shaved her head and the Midas Rex bone saw, which she could not have actually "seen." She was even later able to repeat actual sentences spoken by the team when things went wrong, as when it was determined her arteries were too small on one side of her groin.

At one point, Reynolds's EEG brain waves completely flattened and her heart stopped. Her brain stem became unresponsive, and eventually the team drained her body of blood, pronouncing her clinically dead. That's when Reynolds's OBE turned into a classic NDE and she began having the widely reported visions of the light at the end of the tunnel and seeing dead relatives and friends, including her grandmother, waiting for her. She entered a brilliant and loving light and then was suddenly plunged back into her body when the operating team snipped the aneurysm, turned the bypass machine back on, and began pumping warm blood back into her body, thus bringing her out of death and back into life.

Two hours later, Reynolds was in the recovery room.

She had experienced both the sensation of leaving her physical sense and seeing and hearing things she in no way could have, and then, when she was clinically dead, entering the realm of the near-death experiencer until she was once again fully restored to the living. She walked the Grid, proving to her medical team that these life-changing experiences are absolutely real and defy all logic. How could she, with her eyes and ears sealed, know what was happening and recite later word for word what was spoken? Why did she, like millions of others' experiences documented all over the world, enter into an amazing experience with common themes upon her death and then come back to tell about it, thus corroborating the work of people like American psychiatrist Raymond Moody in his book *Life after Life,* and hundreds of books and studies to follow?

So, what happens after we die? The only clues we have come from those who have died and lived to tell about it.

James and Eben and even Pam Reynolds aren't alone. Every year, thousands of other unique experiences are reported throughout the world by people who all seem to share the same uncanny ability to recall locations, languages, and memories—in vivid detail—of experiences they have never experienced (at least in their current lifetimes). These details often include the same exact process: Seeing a dark tunnel and traveling through it to be met by loved ones, as a bright and loving light envelops you in total goodness or safety. There is a sense of being told to go back and finish what you started; you cannot "die"; then you are sent back through the tunnel, often in a more violent and brusque manner than the way you came in.

Could our brains simply be imagining these images and themes, all a series of simple neural actions designed to make death easier, or is it just a total coincidence? Or are these glimpses into other levels of a multiverse that tells us we will never die or lose our loved ones and that we have a purpose?

In the October 14, 2012, edition of *Psychology Today*, Alex Lickerman writes about the work of psychiatrist Ian Stevenson, who has conducted more than 2,500 case studies over forty years on children who allegedly recall past-life memories. Lickerman reports:

He [Stevenson] methodically documented each child's statements and then identified the deceased person the child identified with, and verified the facts of the deceased person's life that matched the child's memory. He also matched birthmarks and birth defects to wounds and scars on the deceased, verified by medical records such as autopsy photographs. While skeptics have argued his reports provide only anecdotal evidence, his data does seem to demand explanation.

Over the last few decades, more and more of these experiences have involved corroboration, as did Pam Reynolds's time in the operating room.

In *Brain Wars*, Mario Beauregard offers another tantalizing story of a woman named Maria who suffered cardiac arrest and was able to look down on herself and the medical team as she lay on the examining table. She even traveled outside the hospital somehow and saw a tennis shoe on the third floor ledge of the north side of the building. Once she was revived, Maria described the shoe and its location in detail to her critical-care social worker, Kimberly Clark, who found it exactly as Maria had described it. Clark stated that there was no possible way Maria could have ever discerned the shoe without the ability to literally float outside at very close range.

Near-Death and Out-of-Body Experiences

These OBEs and NDEs even happen to blind people, thus proving that the brain does not within its limited constructs hold all of the ability to "see" something. In 1994, researchers Kenneth Ring and Sharon Cooper worked with the blind and found that their NDEs were classic and that they transcended the ability of physical sight. They called this mode of perception "mindsight." Perhaps mindsight allows us to experience the visual aspects of the other levels of the Grid that normally remain outside the abilities of our eyes and brains alone.

Skeptics often claim that these experiences are caused when parts of the brain are compromised, like in the case of the "dying brain" theory, where a lack of oxygen during the dying process may fire off the neurons responsible for visions. But those involved intensely in NDE research counter that if this were the case, every patient who experienced a loss of oxygen would have an NDE, which is not the case. Also, this does not explain the fact that many of the near-death experiencers did not have low oxygen levels at the time of their experience. Normal levels of oxygen were present in the brain at the time, so another factor had to have been present.

Are these just wishful hallucinations? Are they collective visions that are passed on via the media, movies, and books? When we die, or come close to it, do we just automatically expect to see a tunnel and our dead relatives? It is possible, but highly improbable.

What is fascinating, though, is how the patients who come out of an NDE feel afterward—enlightened, empowered, and with a new lease on life. Many have reported having the stark realization that everything is connected and everything matters. They got a vision of the totality of reality and brought it back home to transform their lives with a new understanding of life, death, and what it means to be human.

Indeed, the phenomena of NDEs and OBEs demand an explanation. Experiences such as these also raise the interesting (and quite controversial) question that probably haunts us more than any other: Is death truly the end of our time with our loved ones? Or is it merely the beginning, a rebirth of sorts? Will our souls reconnect along the Grid with other souls we've come to know and love on this level of the Grid?

Regardless of your religious ideology, the question of "what happens next?" is a universal one. Even the most devoutly religious feel the doubt and fear that perhaps their beliefs were wrong, or misinterpreted, upon the moment of death. Yet many cultures celebrate death not so much as an ending, but as a passing over from one world to another, one level to another.

What if we were to look beyond the religious views and dogma of heaven and hell and apply real, testable, scientific principles to help answer this essential question?

The concept of rebirth, or reincarnation, has scientific underpinnings that could make it a legitimate possibility. Surprisingly, science (and not simply religious belief) may be used to help ease our apprehension and fear of death.

First, let's have a quick science lesson. From our knowledge of classical Newtonian science, we know that energy exists in many different forms (heat, light, electrical, chemical, etc.). Electrochemical processes govern our primary biological processes.

When we eat, the chewing process utilizes mechanical energy. Swallowing then utilizes gravitational and muscular energy. As the body then begins to digest our food, it does so using chemical and mechanical energy. Our bodies utilize sugar for energy and generate energy from the digested proteins and fats. Our nerves carry electrical impulses to the brain. Our brains mediate motor (muscular) control via electrical impulses that travel to the muscles, exciting them and causing a reaction.

Scientists have identified four distinct "laws" of thermodynamics that define fundamental physical quantities (temperature, energy, and entropy) that can be used to describe all thermodynamic systems. These laws are used to describe how these quantities behave in different circumstances. For the purposes of this discussion, we are only concerned with the first two laws.

The first law of thermodynamics (conservation) states that energy cannot be created nor destroyed; however, it can change form and move from one area to another. According to this law of nature, the total amount of energy and matter in the universe remains constant. In other words, all of the energy that ever was, is, or will ever be already exists—it merely changes form from one type to another.

The second law of thermodynamics states that in all energy exchanges, the potential energy of the state will always be less than the initial state unless energy enters or leaves the system. This concept is commonly referred to as "entropy." Think of the last time you ran out of gas in your car. Unless you called roadside assistance, the car would not run again until you walked to a gas station and refueled your ride. Once the potential energy from the gasoline is converted to kinetic energy (energy in motion), the mechanism (or organism) will get no more energy until it is input again. That would be a classic example of entropy in action.

Let's go back to entropy for a second. Entropy is actually a measure of disorder. When applied to the human organism, entropy wins when the cells cease to take in energy and subsequently die. But "die" is merely a subjective term, as the energy that comprises the human system would actually transfer to another type of energy upon death of the physical structure. Just because the physical body seems to perish in one form does not mean it is vanishing entirely from the system itself; it may in fact be transferring form to another system, just as physical law dictates.

The concept of "recycling" comes to mind. Perhaps nature's "recycling" of energy might help to explain the thousands of reports similar to James Leininger's, the little boy at the beginning of this chapter who recounted his past lives from a very young age. What if our energy simply recycles upon physical death of the human organism? This introduces a whole different set of logistical issues—mainly "who" we are, and what part of "us" might get recycled. We know that the body returns to the earth, but what of the soul, the spirit, consciousness, and essence?

Dr. Alex Lickerman from *Psychology Today* reflects:

Given what we now know about the enormous size and power of the unconscious—about just how much of "us" lies beneath the surface of our conscious minds—we have to admit that the defining core of who we are may in fact be located mostly, if not entirely, beneath our awareness (our conscious minds being mostly spectators and interpreters of our unconscious selves).

For many, this might be a difficult pill to swallow. While Buddhists believe that the concept of self is actually an illusion created and perpetuated by many variables and factors (both internal and external), most other religious seem to be a bit more ambiguous. Western traditions focus more on the body as well as the spirit, often giving the body characteristics of being less important and more primal and mundane, even "sinful" and capable of sin, while the spirit has the ability to transcend the limitations of the body and move away from primal urges. But we know that the self is more than the body, or the spirit, or the mind; it is a combination of all three, and perhaps then some, as in the idea that we are a piece of a larger puzzle, one with it, yet separate from it enough to have what we deem our own experience of it.

If we aren't even sure what actually defines us as an individual (the "who"), then how would one's "self"—one's memories, beliefs, and experiences—even factor into the equation?

Is the concept of "self" a measurable form of energy? What makes each of us an individual? According to ancient Egyptians, the "soul" was found in the heart, and tomb pictures from around the year 2000 BCE show the god Anubis weighing the soul-laden heart against the feather of truth. This iconic imagery certainly makes one ponder the knowledge that this supposedly "primitive" civilization may have had.

THE SOUL AND THE BRAIN

Fast-forward to 1515, and Leonardo da Vinci had a slightly different idea. Da Vinci believed that the soul was contained within the brain, and when he attempted to find the soul by dissecting the brain he was soon after denounced by many as a sorcerer.

In the modern era, many believe that the soul is distinct from the cognitive areas of the brain. Interestingly, in 1907 an American doctor by the name of Duncan MacDougall conducted experiments where he measured the change in weight of patients who were dying of tuberculosis. MacDougall's research (which to this day remains highly controversial) determined that the body lost twenty-one grams immediately upon physical death. MacDougall hypothesized that this weight loss was the result of the soul leaving the body.

A more intriguing, and modern, look at the soul and how it may relate to near-death experiences comes to us from the world of quantum physics. Dr. Stuart Hameroff, Emeritus Professor in the Psychology and Anesthesiology Departments and Director of the Center for Consciousness Studies at the University of Arizona, proposed a theory with British physicist Sir Roger Penrose based on a "quantum theory of consciousness." By looking at the effects of quantum gravity in microtubules in brain cells, they posited in October 2012 that consciousness may be a program for a quantum computer in the brain that can persist as a part of the universe long after death. This idea mirrors the concept of the field or the Grid as a repository for all energy, form, thought, and action and that what comes from the Grid returns to it upon death. It also mirrors Buddhist and Hindu concepts of consciousness as a part of the universe itself, not separate from it.

Hameroff and Penrose go on to state in their theory, which they call orchestrated objective reduction, or Orch-OR, that we have a soul that is more than just brain activity or the interaction of specific neurons. The soul is a part of the greater fabric of the universe itself, and may even have been around since the beginning of time. This is a stunning admission from two quantum physicists, and more proof that the behavior of reality at the subatomic level is quite different from its behavior on the more visible, grander scale. Yet it gives us amazing insight and clues into the hidden infrastructure that all of reality is a part of.

Hameroff told the Science Channel's Through the Wormhole that even if the heart stops beating and blood stops flowing in the body, these microtubules, which are a component of our cellular infrastructure in the brain, lose their quantum state, but "the quantum information within the microtubules is not destroyed; it can't be destroyed, it just distributes and dissipates to the universe at large." Remember those laws of thermodynamics that describe the inability to destroy energy?

Once a person is resuscitated, Hameroff continues, the quantum information simply goes back into the microtubules and can even give the patient a near-death experience, because, in fact, a part of the person did indeed go beyond the confines of physical death. If the patient is not revived, and thus really "dies," that information will exist outside of the person's body as their "soul."

This amazing and controversial concept is not without its skeptics and detractors, but the scientific community is being forced each and every day to move beyond its limited and empirical views of reality and death and examine the possibility that there really is no such thing as finality to consciousness, to the soul, even though the body itself may not live forever.

Information as energy is the key, as per the holographic view of the brain, where memory and consciousness may be stored outside of the brain and projected upon it from another dimension or source, perhaps the Grid itself. In terms of life beyond death and the survival of consciousness, information, then, might act upon the brain and can exist with or without it, before and after life, simply as a transfer of energy within the system to a different type of energy, or a transfer out of the system into another completely different system.

Death, then, becomes something akin to being in a theater multiplex, where one movie comes to an end and the crowd either goes home or sneaks into another theater to see another movie being projected onto the screen. Different movie, but same multiplex. Different energy, but same system. Or, if you choose to go home and watch TV, different energy, different system. Yes, this is an extreme simplification, but the imagery provides an easy-to-understand illustration of the fact that just because something comes to an end does not mean the whole show is over.

Is the Brain Mind?

Remember our discussion of Karl Pribram, PhD, champion of the holographic brain theory? He posited that the brain implements holonomic transformations that distribute episodic information over regions of the brain, and later "refocuses" them into a form in which we remember. This process occurs on an implicate order (recall David Bohm) in which information is spread out and distributed in a holographic sense. There is, then, a distinct relationship between our perception of "reality" and this process that occurs in the hidden order of reality. This, he points out, is different from the mental processes of thinking, seeing, hearing, and giving our attention to something. Mind may or may not exist, then, depending on exactly how we define mind.

The age-old battle to determine whether the brain and the mind are one and the same, and whether mind/consciousness can outlive physical death, continues, but the more we understand about the brain, the stranger it seems. We know even less about how our consciousness relates to the brain. So to say that we have any kind of proof at all that one exists without the other is impossible, except for subjective, personal experiences of life beyond brain death, and those are getting harder and harder to sweep under the rug—especially when they happen to the very scientists who were once skeptical themselves.

Knowing that we all come from the same thing we return to, and that we are connected, always, via the hidden levels of reality, should make us realize just how precious we are to one another, and how everything we do influences the world around us, like a ripple in a pond, traveling ever outward and changing the pond itself. Yet how often do we treat life as if it's a throwaway, and each other as if we are expendable? It's easy to lose sight of the importance of that deeper connectivity while we are making sure our egos are intact and that we look out for number one.

More than any other experience, death changes us. It removes the physicality we have been bound to in this life and releases a part of us that no sage has yet been able to prove and no scientist has been able to disprove. No matter how complex our brains and bodies are, they do not survive this transition of our core energy, the "information" that is you and me and him and her. That information reenters the field, the sea of quantum possibility and pure potentiality. Nothingness. Until it's time to become something altogether new and different and travel to another level of perceptions and sensations and experiences again.

Death, and what comes before and after it, is simply another floor in the skyscraper, another level of experience and reality, or perhaps even more accurately, the doorway to another level of the Grid.

Part Three

Walking the Grid

CHAPTER 8

STRANDS IN THE WEB

Communicating Information in the Grid

My brain is only a receiver, in the universe there is a core from which we obtain knowledge, strength and inspiration. I have not penetrated into the secrets of this core, but I know that it exists.

—NIKOLA TESLA

Every day I try to be in communication with the universe in an unconscious way.

—PAULO COELHO

There is a transcendental dimension beyond language. . . . It's just hard as hell to talk about!

—TERENCE MCKENNA

If the Grid exists, then it contains information about everything that ever was, is, or will be. Past, present, and future. From matter and form to idea and intent, from the subatomic to the cosmic, everything can be broken down into information. Imagine being able to find a way to tap into this multidimensional and infinitely expansive information field and access what might normally only exist beyond the realm of our five simple senses. Perhaps we are already communicating in the Grid without even knowing it.

INTUITION

In March 2012, the United States Navy announced that it had started a program to investigate how military personnel could be trained to use intuition and their "sixth sense" in combat. The program was inspired by reports from soldiers in Iraq and Afghanistan who reported having some type of unexplained sensation or feeling before they ran into either an enemy attack or an improvised explosive device. The program, called Enhancing Intuitive Decision Making through Implicit Learning, offered $3.85 million to researchers who wanted to explore how intuition works at accessing information that is not clearly available to the other senses or the brain.

In a statement to the press, program manager Ivy Estabrooke stated: "There is a growing body of anecdotal evidence, combined with solid research efforts, that suggests intuition is a critical aspect of how we humans interact with our environment, and how, ultimately, we make many of our decisions."

While critics are quick to point out that intuition does not always work (or does it, and we just read the signals wrong?) and that it is not something we might describe as "paranormal" in nature, most of us have experienced the power of intuition in our own lives, and for many of us, we live by that inner wisdom. It works.

The fact that an entity as formidable as the US Navy might take intuition seriously aside, communicating along the invisible connective web is no longer thought of as a joke (and a big New Age joke at that). Psi, psychic abilities, intuition, remote viewing, precognition, and just plain "knowing" long held court in the realm of the anomalous, and yet we all know these abilities are real. Some of us are even damn good at them.

We get a feeling, a knowing, a gut reaction that may have no grounding in intellectual reality, but we feel it strongly . . . and then it turns out to be true. This knowledge, this information, is bypassing the normal channels of the brain and getting to us on a much different, deeper level. Some researchers say intuition and knowing are really the brain reacting to something based on past experiences and external cues, and that this reaction is happening instantaneously. The March 2008 issue of the *British Journal of Psychology* featured a study on intuition, viewing it as the "instantaneous evaluation of such internal and external cues," which means that this method of communication is a combination of what is outside of us interacting with what is inside. What is on the inside can include memories, past experiences, and learned lessons, but many people swear that their intuition comes from higher sources that have a knowing that goes beyond their own cranial memory and manufacture. Intuition may then be our subconscious at work, prodding us to pay attention to information that the waking brain filters out because it is not rational, or there are no visible external cues to match it with.

In a November 1, 2002, *Psychology Today* article by David Myers titled "The Powers and Perils of Intuition," the author discusses this instinctive awareness buried within us, which reveals a "fascinating unconscious mind that Freud never told us about. Thinking occurs not onstage, but offstage, out of sight." Myers points to how memory, thinking, and even attitude all operate on two different levels: the conscious/deliberate and the unconscious/automatic. This dual processing suggests that we actually know more than we think we know, and that much of our everyday thinking, feeling, and acting operate outside of our conscious awareness: "We have, it seems, two minds: one for momentary awareness, the other for everything else." Many people find it hard to accept this idea.

Intuition may have physiological origins, but it also gives us access to information in the Grid that the brain might normally pass on, or second-guess, or ignore altogether.

TELEPATHY

Telepathy is another way we can access information that the brain and five senses don't normally perceive. Telepathy and ESP have also prompted some serious scientific study, but because it just isn't "provable" and repeatable, it still gets swept under the rug as pseudoscience, along with intuition and knowing. Frederic W. H. Myers, founder of the Society for Psychical Research, coined the term telepathy in 1882, although at the time the phrase "thought transference" was more in vogue to describe the ability to communicate without physical means of contact. The word itself comes from the

Greek *tele* meaning "distant" and *pathe* or *patheia* meaning "feeling, perception, or experience."

Empirical proof of telepathy does not exist, but there are more than enough anecdotal stories of personal experiences, especially between people who have a strong connection to one another, such as twins, lovers, best friends, and parents and their children. One couple, Mark Boccuzzi and Dr. Julie Beischel, authors of an upcoming book called *Psychic Intimacy: A Handbook for Couples,* actually met at a conference and experienced a powerful connection to one another while engaging in an experiment on telepathy! They had their experience during a conference that was organized by the Institute of Noetic Sciences (IONS), where Dr. Dean Radin, author of many books that delve into consciousness and connectivity and the potential science behind it, conducted the study program they were enrolled in. Boccuzzi, Beischel, and Radin cannot prove this happened, but they know it did. How important is subjective experience, and how does it fit into the scientific method, if at all?

And what do we make of the many studies of telepathy between twins? Ask many a twin and you will get a story of some amazing psychic connection between the two, no matter how much distance between them. In her book *Entwined Lives,* Dr. Nancy L. Segal researched twins and their potential psychic connections and concluded that there was no scientific proof of the mental connection claimed by the twins she studied, a conclusion mirrored by that of another twin expert, Dr. Eileen Pearlman. But this does not discount the hundreds, if not thousands, of anecdotal experiences reported all over the world by twins themselves, a phenomenon thought to be more common between identical twins, who share a closer genetic connection than fraternal twins, although all twins report these amazing telepathic communications.

Family members often know when another member is in trouble. Moms know when their children are ill or in danger. A wife knows that her husband, who is a cop, has been shot, or a lover senses that his beautiful adored one is ill. We communicate across the miles without the use of phones or gadgets, one the sender and one the receiver, as if there were invisible phone lines connecting each and every one of us to the other, with the lines much stronger between those we feel a deep love or emotional bond with.

RELATIONSHIPS

Relationships seem to have their own resonance, their own vibration between those involved, and perhaps the resonant frequencies that sync up create this opening for communication in the Grid. Loved ones who have passed on may use this mechanism as a means to communicate with those left behind. Get onto the right wavelength, so to speak, and you can talk to anyone, anywhere, at any time with nothing more than your mind, your consciousness, and your inner voice. The quality of our communication in the Grid may vary in strength or reliability based on, as described in previous chapters, the internal and external influences that either align perfectly, or not. Think of each of us as a radio station broadcasting our own programming, each on our own frequency. We can also receive other frequencies, so we can listen to stations other than our own, and sometimes we even get cross interference and static between signals that are moving in and out of range. Some signals are just beyond our range until we move in a new direction.

We mainly communicate with our brains, which signal to us what to do, say, and think. Then we speak or act and the receiver of our communication hopefully gets the gist of what we are trying to say. Yet the brain is but one mode of communication, and maybe not even the best or most efficient. In a September 12, 2012, article for *Waking Times* titled "The Heart Has Its Own Brain and Consciousness," researchers looked at how consciousness may emerge not just from the brain, but also from the body, mainly the heart. The research was done at the Institute of HeartMath, which is devoted to educating the world about heart-based living and intelligence, and utilized the discipline of neurocardiology to show the heart is a sensory organ that also doubles as a very sophisticated center for the reception and processing of information.

The heart may even be able to make functional decisions about the body independent of the brain, as the heart sends signals to the brain about perception, cognition, and emotional processing. The heart and the brain both have measurable electromagnetic fields, although the heart's field is said to be sixty times stronger. Through an extensive neural communication network the heart and brain are able to interact and communicate. So, though it may seem like we are thinking just on an intellectual level, or communicating thusly, we aren't. This definitely adds so much more meaning to the phrase "heart-to-heart talks."

You can stand several feet away from another person and be affected by their heart's EM field. Perhaps this interaction between heart fields can account for why we sometimes meet someone and click immediately, or hate their guts from the get-go. Our heart may be communicating information to the brain to either say yes or no to a particular person's energetic field. According to the Institute of HeartMath, this may act as a carrier wave for information, thus providing a global synchronization signal for the entire body. Imagine if our global sync signal matches another person, either standing before us or a thousand miles away.

This perspective mirrors both the enfolding and unfolding activities of Bohm's implicate order in the creation of reality, as well as the holographic theory in which the part contains the whole. These heart fields may also occur between humans and animals, which might explain the psychic bonds owners feel with their pets, as well as an animal's ability to detect danger or distress long before its human owner is aware of it.

If we are all energy, and everything is energy, then we simply need to find a way to match our energy with that field of information and send our thoughts to a loved one. This same mechanism may be at work with regards to ESP and remote viewing, which is the uncanny ability to "see" things miles away without aid of actually being there to see it.

ESP AND REMOTE VIEWING

ESP and remote viewing are not just pseudoscientific mumbo jumbo. In fact, both subjects, considered the realm of the paranormal, have been intensely studied in research facilities the world over, with intriguing results. From the early beginnings of organized ESP research, courtesy of the Society for Psychical Research (formed in 1882), to the later attempts by researchers at Stanford University in the early 1900s, the efforts to scientifically prove this hidden, perceptive, and communicative ability have had mixed results. Some of the best research occurred later, in the 1930s at Duke University, when Karl Zener and J. B. Rhine began conducting experiments with Zener cards, which utilized five simple symbols on white cards, to mixed results. Rhine would go on to establish the Parapsychological Association in 1957, which would go on to garner scientific credibility in 1969 when it became a part of the American Association for the Advancement of Science (AAAS).

Later came the Rhine Research Center, IONS, and the famed PEAR program (Princeton Engineering Anomalies Research), where a number of anomalous studies, usually privately funded, were conducted. The PEAR lab is no longer, although its associated Global Consciousness Project continues to operate. More on that later.

Brave researchers and those brilliant minds at IONS, the Rhine Research Center, and other such institutes on the cutting edges of science and human consciousness mostly conduct today's ESP research. Many respected journals continue to publish articles examining ESP, precognition, and telepathy, although proof seems inconclusive.

The term "remote viewing" was coined by Russell Targ and Harold Puthoff, two of the scientists and parapsychology researchers most involved with studying this strange ability to sense the whereabouts of a distant location or the description of a distant object, all without the benefit of actually knowing said location or object. In the 1970s, Targ and Puthoff (who was also instrumental in zero-point field/energy research) became a part of the Electronics and Bioengineering Lab at Stanford Research Institute in Menlo Park, California, where they worked on projects involving laser physics and quantum mechanics. With funding from the Parapsychology Foundation and IONS, they also were able to branch out and conduct research involving ESP and remote viewing. In fact, their studies were instrumental in developing some of the standards and methodology behind all future research.

Even the governments of the world and the military bodies in power have thought enough of ESP and remote viewing to pour significant time and money into research. Russia, China, and the United States have all had top secret "black projects" involving ESP research, and in 1972 the CIA decided to jump into the game with significant funding for a project called Stargate. This particular project initially had a singular purpose: to find any possible military applications for ESP and other psi abilities. However, the program was later expanded with strong support from several top CIA officials. Targ and Puthoff were getting some positive results with remote viewers, namely the talents of Ingo Swann, Pat Price, Rosemary Smith, and Joseph McMoneagle, who actually received a legion of merit for providing critical military information via his remote viewing abilities. Even the PEAR lab at Princeton University had its own Remote Perception program, which ended when the lab itself shut down in 2007.

Funding and government involvement continued through the 1990s and expanded outward to the UK, where they conducted their own studies into remote viewing. The US-backed studies were said to terminate in the mid-1990s, but remote viewing experimentation continues to this day at facilities devoted to not just researching but also actually teaching the art of "seeing at a distance." More recently, cognitive neuroscientist Michael Persinger worked with remote viewing at Laurentian University to examine the accuracy of Ingo Swann's viewings and drawings and the results achieved by forty participants utilizing particular brain stimulation with complex magnetic fields. Persinger is known for his groundbreaking work with the brain and stimulating specific regions to induce creativity, mystical experiences, and altered states using his "God Helmet," which transmits pulses of varying EM frequencies into the brain.

Not everyone is good at remote viewing, or ESP, but some positive findings have prompted research to continue. People like Ingo Swann may have been a ten on a scale from one to ten, but most of us hover around a three or a four. Here's the thing: Remote viewing can be learned, as can any communication in the Grid. If one person has the inherent ability to do something, then it makes sense that we all do, since we all share the same physical parts and potentiality. We can't help but think of the lyrics to that old Who song about having the magic in your eyes to see for miles and miles and miles . . .

COHERENT CONSCIOUSNESS

But there might just be a more collective communication that happens in the Grid as well. Linked consciousness, the collective unconscious, the field of intention . . . these are terms all used to describe a hidden level of connectivity that allows many people to have access to the same information and ideas, often at the same time, as in trends and tipping points.

This collective human consciousness might even influence physical objects, such as random number generators used by the Global Consciousness Project (GCP), which is a collaboration of scientists and engineers who collect data from a network of random number generators at seventy host sites scattered throughout the world (one of which is hosted by coauthor Larry Flaxman!). The director of the GCP is Roger Nelson, PhD, who was previously the coordinator of research at the PEAR lab before moving on to the study of special states of group consciousness using random event generator (REG) technology. The REGs (which are also referred to as RNGs or EGGSs) transmit data 24/7/365 to a central archive. That data is basically the result of the synchronized feelings or emotional energy of millions of people, which somehow influences the random generators' outcomes. All of the readings are recorded and archived for corroboration and study.

The idea behind the GCP is that when a major global event occurs, such as the death of Princess Diana, the 9/11 terrorist attacks, or the Japan tsunami, the collective emotion influences the data of the generators, as if group consciousness is at work. The random data somehow becomes less random. The data often shows that this collective influence occurs immediately preceding the time at which the global event occurs, as if the event were somehow anticipated by huge numbers of people on a hidden order of reality. You may have actually helped to influence one of these REGs and not even consciously realized it. All of this is happening on another level of the Grid, a level where words and actual physical interaction are not necessary for the transmission of information to and from large groups of people.

This concept of "coherent consciousness," as the folks at the GCP call it, finds structure and order in what is ordinarily chaos and disorder. The REGs normally put out random orders of zeroes and ones, but when a major event occurs in the world, those zeroes and ones take on a subtle order, a pattern that is undeniable. The bigger the event, the more patterns are seen in the data. This seems to be especially true when the events evoke a deep compassion or empathy among the populace. Strong emotions make an imprint upon the REGs, but interestingly, the emotion of strong fear creates smaller effects than that of compassion. It is as if minds, and hearts, everywhere were talking to one another without mouths ever moving. The evidence accumulated by REGs over time has shown that there is an interconnected human consciousness at work that can affect and influence the GCP instrumentation, which in turn may also be influencing reality itself.

COLLECTIVE INTENTION

A similar undertaking involves the use of collective intention, or focused thought, to change reality and influence objects from a distance. Lynne McTaggart, author of *The Field* and *The Intention Experiment,* has a website devoted to intention experiments that are scientifically controlled, Web-based, and open to public participation. As of the writing of this book, there have been several intention experiments involving more than thirty countries around the world, and the website claims extraordinary results so far.

The very first experiment had its trial run on March 11, 2007, using the attendees of one of McTaggert's own conferences in London. Dr. Gary E. Schwartz, a psychologist and director of the Laboratory for Advances in Consciousness and Health at the University of Arizona, coordinated the experiment. In it, two healthy geranium leaves were taken from a plant belonging to one of Dr. Schwartz's office colleagues. The audience then sent one leaf directed intention for ten minutes, telling it to "glow and glow." This attempt to increase the light emissions of the leaf was photographed using a CCD camera. The other leaf didn't receive any directed intention and was used as a control. A week later, Dr. Schwartz revealed the results. The leaf sent the glowing intention had such strong changes in light emissions it could easily be seen in the camera's digital images.

Similar experiments involving water crystals, plants, and even germinating seeds have been conducted, but one of the biggest involved peace. The Peace Intention Experiment marked the tenth anniversary of 9/11 and was intended to be a positive impact event during a very depressing, downbeat time. The experiment attracted participants from more than seventy-five nations and lasted for eight days, during which people focused their intention on communion, solidarity, and peace between the East and the West.

Though measuring actual declines in violence in the most tense, war-ridden areas of the world proved tough, eventually it was revealed that for the month of September and the few months following, the overall violence, the number of civilian and military deaths in Iraq and Afghanistan, and the number of attacks by the Taliban were all down. The exact numbers are available on the Intention Experiment website (http://theintentionexperiment.com). Some of the summary points of interest include:

◎ Civilian casualties dropped 37 percent after the September intention.

- Overall enemy attacks dropped 12 percent between October and December of 2011.

- Explosive device attacks dropped 16 percent during the intention period as compared with the previous two years.

- Attacks throughout Afghanistan were down 9 percent from 2010 levels.

Can this be used as proof that the participants actually changed reality with their focused thoughts? Not necessarily, but the ongoing work that McTaggart, her researchers, and the Global Consciousness Project are doing is certainly intriguing.

The Institute of HeartMath calls this phenomenon in which the social collective becomes both the activator and regulator of the energy in a social system a "social field." There is an energetic field present that connects the positively, or negatively, charged emotions of all the members of a social group, creating a coherent organization. In addition, this network of emotions in the energetic field is encoded with information about the group's social structure, information that can then be distributed throughout the group, as in collective intention and action.

It's as if our minds and hearts and consciousness are entangled and forever influenced by one another, and in a quantum sense that is entirely possible. Entanglement of particles, we know from the quantum world, creates a connection that can be measured even over vast distances. As two particles become entangled with one another, even if they are a billion miles away, they will react to each other's influence instantaneously, even suggesting that light speed does not apply to this spooky "action at a distance," as Einstein referred to it.

Non-locality, which is often mistaken for entanglement, tells us that two objects can be in non-local environments and still have an immediate influence upon one another. Though physicists still hotly debate the details of both entanglement and non-locality, the general understanding holds that when you measure the property of one entangled particle, you can automatically know the property of the other entangled particle. It's as if these particles communicate with each other instantly, with no thought of how far away they are from one another at all, defying the light speed limitations we hold so dear in physics.

You might be thinking, so what if this happens at the quantum level? Big deal. We are not particles (although we *are* made up of them!). Yet the February 15, 2013, issue of *Science* magazine features a joint experiment with the University of Colorado, Boulder and the National Institute of Standards and Technology (NIST) that may blow that whole quantum limitation out of the water. The physicists placed a tiny drum between two mirrors and then illuminated it with laser light. When the mirrors were shaken, it was distinctly clear that effects of the uncertainty principle of quantum physics, which states that one cannot measure both a particle's momentum and its position at the same time, were present, thus suggesting that what works at the quantum level may work at the cosmic level as well. That was what made this experiment so stunning, that the results showed both classical and quantum mechanics operating on the very same scale. The fact that nothing really has a fixed form until we observe it may not just apply to particles anymore, but to objects on a much larger scale—even us!

Could our consciousness be entangled in a similar way, causing a virtual hidden communications field by which we transmit and receive information in the Grid? Dr. Dean Radin's *Entangled Minds: Extrasensory Experiences in a Quantum Reality* and *The Conscious Universe: The Scientific Truth of Psychic Phenomena* both address his research into this deeper reality, where the effects of microscopic entanglements "scale up" into the macroscopic world. Radin also writes extensively about how human consciousness is critical to our understanding of reality and how psi abilities, which were once thought to be the realm of fringe science, make perfect sense in light of the concept of a universe as an interconnected whole.

Entangled minds would definitely explain things like trends, memes, ideas, and concepts that go viral, suggesting that even our minds are subject to contagion just as our bodies are. Viral thought may be what causes tipping points that literally shift entire paradigms in our society, thus creating a ripe time for change on a larger, even global, scale.

In *The Conscious Universe* Radin suggests that rather than looking at the mind as a "mechanistic, information-processing bundle of neurons" or a "computer made of meat" we instead focus on the aspects of mental functioning that seem to go beyond just the normal neural functions of the brain.

Then again, maybe the universe itself is just one big giant computer, and we are all just information being processed by some master programmer. The idea of some giant cosmic computer behind all of reality is not new and is actually taken quite seriously by physicists who seek proof that we might all be living in a giant simulation. The idea that our universe exists within a computer simulation, à la the famous 1999 movie *The Matrix*, has been popular among scientists who are seeking the signatures of a cosmic computer model. Researchers at both Cornell University and the University of Washington have been embarking on a viable method of testing this, as reported in December 2012 by Eric Pfeiffer in "Whoa: Physicists Testing to See if Universe Is a Computer Simulation." Physics professor Martin Savage discussed the use of a technique called lattice quantum chromodynamics for simulating a model of a computer, albeit one only slightly larger than the nucleus of an atom. But, the same principles may apply to something on a more cosmic scale. "If you make the simulations big enough, something like our universe should emerge," Savage said.

One of Savage's students took the whole theory one step further by asking the bazillion dollar question: If whoever made our simulated universe may have made others, can we communicate with those other universes if they are running on the same platform? Think about it. Parallel simulated universes, all created by the masterful genius of someone or something with the brilliance to create cosmos. This brings the whole intelligent design argument into play, or the theory of the universe as a giant brain or consciousness, and yes, there are even scientists researching that possibility.

THE UNIVERSAL BRAIN

Could the universe be a giant brain, with the actual electrical firings between brain cells mirrored by the more cosmic firings that shape galaxies and worlds? A group of physicists at the University of California, San Diego think that may be possible. They ran a computer simulation to show natural growth dynamics of evolving systems, and found it to be the same for any kind of network, whether it's the Internet, the brain, or the entirety of reality. The universe shows the same kind of growth as the brain does, in terms of how links and connections evolve. But that doesn't mean the universe thinks like a brain does.

Which brings up this interesting thought: What if reality, and all the levels of the Grid, were like a giant Internet, say a human-driven Internet, with Web-like connections reaching in every possible direction, linking us all to one another, all the time?

The Internet allows us to access the entire world right at our fingertips, with nothing but a few keystrokes and an idea of what and where to search. We can communicate via email, social networks, online texting, and Skype. If we want to learn more about a subject, we do a search for it, and behold, the answer is there almost instantly. If we want to find old friends, we look on Facebook or LinkedIn, and hopefully they haven't changed their names or identities too much. If we want to find new friends, or even dates, there are thousands of places we can look for people we never even knew existed.

All of this is designed to expand our perception of reality, because until we actually search for something, it is not a part of our reality. It isn't "there." But once we sign on and log on and hook up, it becomes a new experience and a new part of how we view the world around us.

Social networking sites like Facebook offer a great analogy for the communication of information in the Grid. People sign up for Facebook usually with the intent of connecting with family and friends, which become level one of reality in the social networking universe. But soon, friends of family and friends of friends are friending us, and now our reality is growing and expanding. This is level two. Maybe then we start a fan page or a business page and befriend a whole different set of people with different interests. This is level three. Until we actively become aware of and participate in the creation of these new outlets, or levels, those people don't exist in our reality. When things go viral, it's because the collective has synchronized and created level four. This is how we share innovations, inventions, ideas, and discoveries that affect the reality of everyone involved. Heck, you can even block someone or a bunch of people on Facebook and rearrange your social reality once again! Maybe this is level five. And the levels continue on and on from here.

The mind-blowing technology of today has made it possible to sign on to a social networking site, post a message, and within seconds that message is responded to by people all over the world. It's as close to instantaneous information transmission as we can get, and we never even question how our message goes through the phone via wireless communications to show up on some scrolling wall literally the nanosecond we tap the "post status" button. Why then is it so hard to believe we are communicating like this on our own, over some wireless frequency that connects brain to brain, heart to heart, soul to soul, no cell phone or computer needed?

Whether we prefer social networking or just surfing the human Internet, the perception of our reality literally shifts with the new knowledge and information we are given access

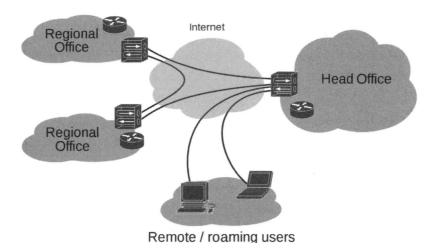

Figure 9. The levels of the Grid may work like a host computer that is sending and receiving data from a network of other terminals. *Courtesy of Ludovic.ferre/Wikimedia Commons*

to. Until we are exposed to these new ideas and bits of information, *they do not exist in our reality.*

When we find ways to communicate via the Grid, whether we are sending or receiving information, wisdom, knowledge, or inspiration, we are acting as a computer that is hooked up to a vast network that is constantly evolving as we put more into it. We may be limited in what we can fit in our own computer's memory, but we still have access to other computers. We may forward files, delete images, add software, or increase memory and basically alter the reality of our computer world constantly throughout the day, according to our needs. If we have a webcam, we can see people we've never met in person. With Skype and other programs we can get on a conference call with twenty other people from all over the world to learn about something we previously didn't have an understanding of.

Our world is so small until we flick the on switch, and then it becomes all about finding the right broadcasts and frequencies that resonate with us.

THE HUMAN INTERNET

The ability to reach across phenomenally vast distances to find something we never knew existed is what the Internet is all about. The human Internet, the experience of our reality in the Grid, operates the very same way. Next time you turn on your computer and Google a YouTube video, or check in on Twitter, or accept a new friend on Facebook, remember, you are creating new levels of reality where none existed before.

Mind to mind, brain to brain, heart to heart, computer to network, whether we are creating reality or are stuck in some virtual simulation, we still have the understanding that our five senses alone are not adequate for all the ways we communicate. Intuition, instinct, knowing, psi, remote viewing, channeling, mediumship, going into a trance state to access other levels of consciousness, or even taking a strange shamanic brew can all serve to help us experience other realities and communicate with those who exist there. When it comes to communication, we are stuck in the rational, intellectual world of visual cues and words, words, words, but perhaps the greatest and most profound levels of communication we can experience are the ones our brains filter out, or cannot perceive without a little help from our sixth sense.

Consciousness seems to have its own language, as does the

collective unconscious that acts as a field of information we can all tap into, and all dump our own stuff into as well (good or bad!). Looking beyond the normal means of transmitting information, we can begin to see that there are "voices" and "signs" all around us at any given time and any given point in space—we just have to know where, and how, to find them. If our consciousness is that much a part of our experience of reality, or perhaps reality itself, then linked consciousness and group meditation or intention aren't so hard to grasp. Maybe, as Lynne McTaggart and Roger Nelson believe, there is a power to this collective that can affect and influence to heal or reduce crime or bring peace to hostile places.

In the end, we are all entangled, whether by six degrees of separation or just a few strands in the web of all there is. And because of that, we all have the ability to reach out and touch someone without ever laying a hand on them, even if it's just with our thoughts and our intentions. If we are observing reality into existence in a singular sense, then we are doing it collectively as well, and forever entwining and entangling ourselves until we get to a point where there is no distinct separation.

In the next and final chapter, we will look at how we ourselves are the Grid, how we can learn to walk the many levels and experience other realities for ourselves, and why it is important that we understand that our perception of reality is flawed, and the truth is so much grander and more awesome than we think. It's an idea that has been around forever, as we have shown, but it's an idea whose time has truly come.

CHAPTER 9

WALKING THE GRID

How We Can Experience Other Levels of Reality

You and I are all as much continuous with the physical universe as a wave is continuous with the ocean.
—ALAN WATTS, *THE NATURE OF CONSCIOUSNESS*

One in All
All in One—
If only this is realized,
No more worry about your not being perfect
—EDWARD CONZE, *BUDDHIST SCRIPTURES* (175)

Quantum physics thus reveals a basic oneness of the universe.

—ERWIN SCHRODINGER

If you have experienced any kind of paranormal, anomalous, or psychic phenomena, you have walked another level of the Grid. Some people have just the right inner and outer influences aligning at the right times in the right places to experience altered states of awareness and get these glimpses of the Grid, but most of us have to work at it. To change conscious awareness of one's reality can be as simple as getting out in nature or working on a project that makes time stand still.

ALTERING YOUR BRAIN WAVE STATE

Altering our brain waves via meditation, chanting, drumming, or even hypnosis allows us to access another part of reality that our waking state must set aside as we go through our day. On a daily basis, our brain cycles through five distinct states:

- ◎ Gamma (more than 40 Hz) The most rapid brain wave frequency, when the brain experiences a burst in learning or information processing at a high level.

- ◎ Beta (13–40 Hz) The state of normal waking alertness. Heightened mental activity and concentration. Maximum mind power. All five external senses, logical mind, memory from the five senses, and logical thinking.

- ◎ Alpha (8–12 Hz) A relaxed state of alertness. Good for inspiration, problem solving, and learning, as well as awareness and reflection. A meditative mind.

- ◎ Theta (4–8 Hz) Deep meditation and relaxation. Light sleep and dreaming. Deep inward thought. High state of mental concentration. The mind during meditation and visualization. Intuition, inner guidance. Access to unconscious information.

- ◎ Delta (0.5–4 Hz) Deep, dreamless sleep. Deep relaxation. State of oneness and pure being, even healing, even deep meditation.

Brain Wave Syncing

A whole new world of brain wave technology has opened up, designed to entrain the brain to improve health, learning, and even healing. The idea is to empower the brain and literally "train" it to think and perceive differently and access the various brain waves that can bring about enlightenment, knowledge, wisdom, and well-being. Also known as brain wave syncing, there are a number of devices on the market that can be used during the sleep cycle or the waking state to align brain waves for the purpose of entrainment. Often these devices use light and sound to alter brain frequencies, or present the brain with pulses or beats that bring about more dual-hemisphere processing.

Binaural beats, the brainchild of a Prussian physicist and meteorologist named Heinrich Wilhelm Dove in 1839, occur when you play two sound waves that are close in frequency, one into each ear, and the brain perceives the beat frequency difference. For example, if you play a 500 Hz tone into one ear and a 515 Hz tone into the other, the binaural beat frequency the brain will perceive is 15 Hz. The ears don't actually hear these tones; only the brain does as it resolves the difference between the two tones presented to it. These binaural beats have been claimed to lead to better learning, improved memory, even healing, as well as shifting the state of awareness in the user.

Other types of tones that claim to have the same affect include modulating sound waves that embed a brain wave

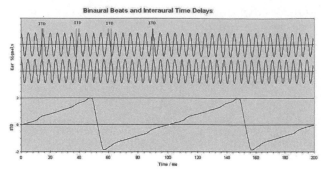

Figure 10. Each ear receives a signal, but the brain perceives the difference in frequencies between the two signals, as in the bottom line, the ITD, or interaural time delay. *Courtesy of SkyheardE/Wikimedia Commons*

entrainment frequency in the track; light and sound entrainment involving beats/tones and flashes of light; bilateral sound machines and Hemi-Syncs that help the two halves of the brain get more in sync; and isochronic tones, which are tones that are evenly spaced and turn on and off, producing a strong reaction in the brain's cortical region. There are machines that can cause increasingly vivid dreams by producing specific frequencies of sound and light before sleep, and machines that can stimulate the cranium itself to generate various brain activities.

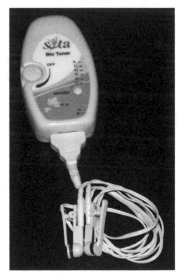

There are devices on the market, some as simple as a pair of headphones, that will produce these beats and tones. The idea again is to present sound fre-

Figure 11. Biotuner
Courtesy of Larry Flaxman

Figure 12. Zapper
Courtesy of Larry Flaxman

quencies to the brain that create patterned activity and shift the brain wave state into a more productive, creative, or meditative mode.

Drumming

While they generally do not utilize technology to achieve their means, shamans use a similar methodology to alter their conscious states and journey into other levels of reality. Drumming and rattling offer the brain a repetitive pattern that can create a trance-like state, allowing the shaman to slip out of waking state consciousness and into another realm where the spirit is free to travel anywhere it wants and meet with a variety of entities that do not exist in the normal reality.

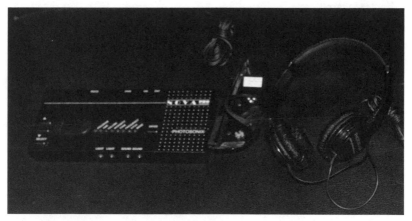

Figure 13. SOVA *Courtesy of Larry Flaxman*

Walking the Grid 159

Drumming is played at a tempo of three to four beats per second (bps) and is sometimes accompanied by another instrument designed to amplify the trance quality of the sound, such as a didgeridoo, musical bow, or even a chorus of deep voices. The timbre, volume, and tempo of the drumming are critical to the achievement of a state of consciousness that allows the shaman to journey or shape shift and enter other levels of the Grid.

Variation in the tone and timbre throughout the journeying adds to the deeper levels that the shaman can enter and guides him or her through different levels of reality, arousing and transmitting just the right energy depending on the purpose of the shaman's journey. In a sense, the drumming sets the stage for the shaman's communication with various entities in these realities, changing as the entities themselves change, and altering not just the vibrational state of the reality the shaman wishes to enter, but the shaman's own vibrational state as well.

Chanting

Chanting and dancing are also means of achieving a trance-like state, even rocking the body back and forth in a rhythmic motion, especially during prayer or meditation practices. Chanting is often described as a type of vocal meditation or repetitive prayer, as it can involve speaking a mantra or part of a religious or sacred text over and over again. Chants can be sung as well as spoken and are a part of many religious practices all over the world. One of the most famous spiritual chanting techniques is the throat singing of Tibetan Buddhist monks, where they are able to achieve multiple frequencies of sound from their singular vocal chords, making one man sound like a chorus!

Chanting doesn't have to be only ritualistic or spiritual, as we see every year during sports games when crowds chant their favorite player's name or team name, creating a heightened energy wave that sweeps everyone into it with its infectiousness. Or ask anyone who has ever been to a rave, where the music pounds in a deep, rhythmic, base-heavy pulse, and lights flash in patterns in sync with the music. The brain goes into an altered state and the body seems to just follow along, responding to the constant sound and light until the patterns change and the brain "wakes up" for a bit, before entering a new trance to a new song.

Even pounding the pavement can cause such an altered state, something many runners will testify to when they get the sought-after runner's high, as endorphins rush to the brain and create a sense of being in the zone. A ride on a motorcycle on a warm summer day can evoke the same feeling, as can getting lost in a good book, or even lying on the beach listening to the sound of the waves and surf.

Athletes, writers, musicians, and artists all know this zone as a place where time slows or stops and focus is so intense that a sense of separateness ceases to exist. Being in the flow is another way to describe this sensation of being a part of a bigger picture, or a drop in a larger river, where the ego of self is set aside for a while and we feel like we really are immersed in the Grid.

Hypnosis

Hypnosis is another way to work with brain waves to either retrieve information or cause behavioral changes, such as stopping smoking or losing weight. Hypnosis can alter consciousness, taking the subject into an altered level of awareness while still remaining awake. The hypnotic state is not a sleep state, and some researchers suggest it is not even really a consciousness state, but perhaps a division or dissociation of consciousness into two parts, the responder and the observer. Medical hypnosis involves the use of a droning voice, flashing lights, or repetitive sounds to induce the proper state. People under hypnosis are highly suggestible and will even forget what they are told under hypnosis if they are told to. This is called posthypnotic amnesia. But being "put under" is a mild glimpse of another reality the brain can experience as it shifts in and out of various states.

Hypnosis can be learned, although the most effective way is with a professional at the helm, which allows the person being hypnotized to fully relax and participate.

Prayer and Meditation

We walk the Grid with devices and without; however, one of the most effective ways is through prayer and meditation. Prayer can mean something different to many people depending on their religious background, but a nice way to think about it is that in prayer we get quiet and go within and talk to our higher source, whatever that may be, and in meditation we get quiet and go within and listen for the answers. Both require a focus of thought and a stillness of mind, although prayer is more active as specific intentions are being put forth into a brain that is in its most receptive state.

Prayer can take the form of a trancelike experience if it involves singing, chanting, rocking, or any other physical act that uses sound and repetition to create the most conducive mental state. Although people pray all the time, such as at ballgames when they want their team to hit a home run, we are talking about deep, intense, sacred prayer here, in which someone actually transcends their body in a sort of heart to heart or mind to mind discussion with something greater than themselves. Some of the most effective prayer involves a particular environment or surrounding, such as a sacred church or a candle-filled room, even a beautiful garden free of distractions.

Meditation is a much more powerful way to access altered states of being and see other potential levels of the Grid simply because it does not involve asking or requesting anything, as prayer does. The spiritual practice of mystics, gurus, and yogis, meditation requires a quieting of the mind and a gentle passing of thought to get to a point of stillness where a sense of oneness and expansion is obtained. Though quieting the mind can be work at first, it is passive, and many people who meditate regularly and deeply report not just a sense of well-being and renewed energy, but the experience of intuition, guidance and insight from higher beings or the higher part of the self that the brain does not consult with during normal waking state activities.

During meditation, the brain actually enters deeper brain wave states, such as theta, and if you are really good at it, delta. Meditation allows you to set aside the rational, intellectual processing in favor of heightened awareness, deeper relaxation, and even slowed pulse and heartbeat as the body responds in kind. Relaxation techniques such as deep breathing, yoga, biofeedback (using your own brain waves to control bodily functions, such as pulse and breathing), and even daydreaming can often achieve the same sense of deeply focused awareness and expansion, although those options don't seem to offer the potential for associated psychic or spiritual experience, as some meditation devotees report, experiences that include out-of-body travel, astral projection, hallucinations and visions, or mystical highs.

Siddhartha Gautama, the Buddha, was said to have achieved spiritual enlightenment while in meditation beneath a Bodhi Tree. Meditation has its roots in ancient Eastern traditions, dating as far back as 1000 BCE as described in the recorded religious texts of Northern India. Meditation was then considered an ecstatic experience, but it was not limited to India. Taoist, Hindu, and even Kabbalistic sacred literature all discuss the importance of a meditation practice, usually a very distinct and serious one as compared to today's rather simple "get quiet and sit" form, in the pursuit of the highest forms of enlightenment and oneness, as well as escape from the limitations and bondages of the external world.

Often meditation involves the use of a mantra, a specific sound, visual symbol, or short phrase that helps to entrain the brain into the right wave state needed for a deep experience of relaxation and openness. Like chanting, drumming, and binaural beats, a mantra serves as a tool for getting the brain wave frequencies to the proper ranges for experiencing the most beneficial meditative experience, one in which even healing of a physical ailment might take place.

Psychoactive Drugs

Altered states of mind that lead to the experience of other realities are most prominent with the use of a variety of psychoactive drugs, both natural and chemically manufactured. These drugs affect the psychology of a person, not just their body, and are often illegal despite their key ingredients being found in nature.

Psychoactive drugs are broken into four groups:

- Stimulants. These drugs stimulate the central nervous system and cause such effects as euphoria and altered consciousness: cocaine, crystal meth, various amphetamines, nicotine, and caffeine.

- Sedatives. These drugs sedate the central nervous system and are also known to cause euphoric states and even hallucinations and a sense of being out of the body: barbiturates, valium, Xanax, alcohol, and marijuana.

- Narcotics. These drugs relieve pain and are often abused to get high or feel a sense of well-being, often even euphoria: morphine, heroin, opium and opiate derivatives, and painkillers like Vicodin.

- Hallucinogens. These drugs actually distort and shift our perception and can affect our vision and hearing: LSD, mescaline, psilocybin mushrooms, salvia, ayahuasca, peyote, and other "natural" blends often used by shamanic and indigenous people to achieve altered states.

The idea behind taking some type of legal or illegal drug is to achieve a euphoric state of being free from the confines of the physical body, as in the classic LSD trip of the shamanic visioning after imbibing ayahuasca, which contains a natural form of DMT found in the *psychotria viridis* plant. The leaves are mixed into a concoction with *Banisteriopsis caapi*, also known as *caapi or yajé*, a South American jungle vine of the family *Malpighiaceae*. These drugs have a direct and powerful influence on the functioning of neurotransmitters and literally change the chemistry of the brain for the duration of their effects.

Psilocybin mushrooms are fungi containing psychoactive indole alkaloids. Approximately 190 species of psilocybin mushrooms have been consumed and used in native and religious rites over the course of history, even as far back as prehistoric times, when they were simply eaten as a source of food. They are considered psychedelics for their influence on the brain and their ability to cause visions, hallucinations, and euphoria, as well as the experience of other states of being or reality.

Salvia Divinorum is another psychoactive plant found in nature that is known to cause visions and hallucinatory experiences. People on salvia have often reported a sense of being out of body and existing in another dimension, even meeting with entities as they move through various states of consciousness. Salvia is used ritually by some shamanic peoples but has also become very popular with modern users eager to experience a dissociative effect that takes them far beyond their physical boundaries.

Peyote, a small cactus plant native to southern Texas and Mexico, contains psychoactive alkaloids like mescaline that when ingested can result in visions, clarity of mind, altered consciousness, even out-of-body experiences. Peyote ceremonies are sacred rituals that are carefully supervised due to the nature of this natural substance to open the inner eye to other realities and even access information from beyond the limitations of the body and mind to heal and help others.

In no way are we advocating experimentation with drugs of any kind, legal or illegal, manmade or natural, but these are viable methods of walking other levels of reality in the Grid, which is why they have been used for hundreds of years, if not more, by tribal peoples who lived close to the earth and understood the power of nature.

INDUCING AN OUT-OF-BODY EXPERIENCE YOURSELF

Having an out-of-body experience does not require drugs. With a lot of practice, you can learn to leave the physical plane. Sometimes people have even done this involuntarily. Like déjà vu, leaving the body and traveling around the non-physical planes of existence tend to happen when they want to or during a negative and scary situation, such as surgery or a car accident. But there are steps you can take to increase the likelihood of having an OBE. Robert Monroe, founder of the Monroe Institute, which is devoted to the study of consciousness, wrote a book called *Journeys Out of the Body* and states that the body will begin to vibrate right before an OBE.

To have your own experience, Monroe suggests doing the following: Find a room that is warm where you won't be disturbed. Wear loose clothing, and remove any jewelry or metal objects. Dim the lights and lie down with your body pointing magnetic north. Relax and repeat five times, "I will consciously perceive and remember all that I encounter during this relaxation procedure. I will recall in detail when I am completely awake only those matters which will be beneficial to my physical and mental being."

Breathe through a half-open mouth, and hopefully you will enter the hypnagogic state between waking and sleep, which alone is ripe for the experience of altered realities and hallucinations, both visual and auditory. Try to stay in this in-between state by lifting your arm and then when it falls upon sleep, the body will jerk awake again until you can stay just on the border of sleep. You can also try focusing on a thought or object in your mind.

Once you reach this in-between state, deepen the experience by observing your field of vision through your closed eyelids, looking for light patterns against the blackness. Once these light patterns stop, suggesting an end to neural discharges in the brain, you must relax even deeper into what is called Condition D, the proper state for leaving the body. With closed eyes, look at a spot in the blackness of your vision about a foot from your forehead, and then begin to move that spot gradually further away, until you achieve a vibrational state, during which the sense of being out of the body will begin.

OK, if this is all too hard and confusing, you can just try relaxing to some soft music and let your mind drift until you feel like you are all mind, entirely mind. No matter the technique, and there are many out there, OBEs provide a great way to experience another level of the Grid from the safety of your own bed, or couch, or lounge chair.

Dreaming

Dreams are wonderful examples of other realities. If you've ever awakened from a nightmare covered in sweat, or dreamt of being chased and had sore legs the next morning, or been sure that you were falling and awakened with a jolt right out of bed, you have experienced how the brain and body see no difference between the dream state and the awakened state. Both realities feel equally real while they are being experienced. Only when we awaken later and wonder why we dreamt of a purple pony or a talking doorknob do we question the reality of our dream state!

Sleep deprivation, on the other hand, can lead to a similar OBE state, as well as hallucinations and the experience of not being grounded in this particular reality. Just ask any new parents!

Lucid dreaming allows the dreamer to control of the outcome of their dreams, which is an interesting way to feel as though you exist in two dimensions at once. Think of being conscious while unconscious, in a reality that is just as real to your mind and body as the waking state is. Being "awake in a dream" is a powerful and exciting experience, and there are ways to improve your chances of having a lucid dream, and controlling your actions and outcomes to your own desires.

One of the best ways to have a lucid dream is to relax right before sleeping and repeat to yourself, "I will have a lucid dream, and I will be aware and awake and in control" or something similar until you fall asleep. Some lucid dreamers journal before sleep, writing down what they want to experience and remember.

Another technique involves counting as you try to enter sleep, such as "One, I am dreaming, two, I am dreaming, three . . ." until you are counting while in the dream itself. Key, though, is affirming your desire to lucid dream before you go to sleep, and maybe even suggesting what it is you want to explore or experience once you do. These types of lucid dream incubation techniques set the mind's expectation to have the experience once the dream state has initiated, and with practice, you can become a regular lucid dreamer.

A quick search online will reveal a number of devices that purport to assist one in lucid dreaming. Seems there's a device for everything nowadays, and it's only a matter of time before someone develops a Gridwalking machine! Do your research and look at reviews of products, and have some discernment; there are many people out there willing to sell you anything if you're willing to buy it. Visiting lucid dream websites and forums and even joining a Facebook group may lead to great ideas, suggestions, and advice for increasing your ability to control your dream destiny!

Sensory Deprivation

One of the most powerful ways to experience an altered reality is to completely deprive the brain of all sensory perceptions. Sensory deprivation experimentation goes all the way back to the 1930s when psychologist Wolfgang Metzger had volunteer subjects gaze into a featureless field of vision until the brain activity changed and they began to hallucinate. This is what is referred to as the ganzfeld effect, a type of perceptual deprivation that involves the brain reacting to an undifferentiated field of one color, usually blackness. Deprived of any reference to anything but the uniform field, the brain begins to see nothing and eventually will hallucinate and enter a different state of brain wave activity and even consciousness.

Later, sensory deprivation experiments involved floating in chambers filled with water. Once the door to the chamber was closed, no light or sound could enter, creating an effect similar to taking hallucinogenic drugs. Without sensory patterns, the brain will begin to create its own, thus the hallucinations, delusions, and even complex visions often reported during sensory deprivation experiments. In the October 2009

Figure 14. A modern sensory deprivation floatation chamber. *Courtesy of FloatGuru/Wikimedia Commons*

issue of *Wired* magazine, reporter Hadley Leggett examined the research of psychologist Paul Fletcher of the University of Cambridge in an article titled "Out of LSD? Just 15 Minutes of Sensory Deprivation Triggers Hallucinations." Fletcher worked with nineteen healthy volunteers in a sensory deprivation room devoid of any light and sound for fifteen minutes at a time. Many of the volunteers began to report hallucinations, depression, and even paranoia. Fletcher later wrote, "It appears that, when confronted by a lack of sensory patterns in our environment, we have a natural tendency to superimpose our own patterns." Because the brain misidentifies the source of what it is experiencing, called "faulty source monitoring," the brain then creates its own source. These sensory deprivation experiences have been likened to those of people taking psychosis-inducing drugs and may even increase the risk of developing psychosis if the deprivation goes on long enough.

The brain, it seems, when exposed to nothing, will create its own reality complete with images and sensations the body itself is not actually feeling or seeing. We hate a blank slate and will do anything to fill it.

Other Methods

Walking the levels of the Grid can occur in so many ways, even those that we call supernatural, such as seeing a ghost or a UFO, having a psychic experience with someone, or encountering a strange creature on a dark road with glowing red eyes. But we are more concerned here with ways we can walk of our own volition and experience other realities intertwined with our own. All it takes is finding the right connectors, triggers, and mechanisms to assist us in perceiving what lies just beyond the confines of our brains and bodies and the capacity of our five senses.

Other potential means of altering our reality can happen during sex; panic; peak experiences, such as running and being in the zone; daydreaming; listening to music; delirium; hysteria; ecstasy; and even religious fervor. It seems our lives are already filled with various ways we shift from one reality to another, often involuntarily.

With practice, anyone can learn to walk the Grid voluntarily. For now, just remember when you go to sleep tonight, you'll be leveling up (or down, as the case may be). Enjoy the reality shift!

Conclusion

We Are the Grid . . .
And Why It Matters

To see reality is as simple as to see one's face in a mirror.
Only the mirror must be clear and true. A quiet mind,
undistorted by desires and fears, free from ideas and
opinions, clear on all the levels, is needed to reflect the
reality. Be clear and quiet, alert and detached, all else will
happen by itself.

—Sri Nisargadatta Maharaj, *I Am That*

There are no extra pieces in the universe. Everyone is
here because he or she has a place to fill, and every piece
must fit itself into the big jigsaw puzzle.

—Deepak Chopra

On a daily basis, we are bombarded with news stories about
people hurting other people, destroying the environment, and
doing harm to other creatures. Greed, selfishness, narcissism,

and violence are the order of the day. It often seems that it is each man for himself. We live in a bubble of our own separateness, groping and grabbing for what we can get before the other guy gets it all.

Over the last year and a half, both authors of this book lost loved ones. In Marie's case, her father passed away after a long battle with ALS (Lou Gehrig's disease). In Larry's case, both his father and mother left this level of the Grid within months of each other. Through our grief and mutual attempts to understand and recalibrate our lives after such significant losses, we both realized something important: We were receiving messages from our loved ones on the other side.

In Marie's case, Larry knew the exact moment of her father's death and actually tried to call and text her at that very same moment, asking her if she was OK. It was approximately 12:30 in the afternoon, and Marie wouldn't find out until hours later that her father had died at that very time. How did Larry know, at exactly 12:30, to try to call and text Marie? Why did he feel an overwhelming sense of doom and a "disturbance in the force," enough so that Marie actually was prompted to inquire about her father's health and discover that he had indeed died?

Larry's parents died within months of each other. His experiences since then have given him the firm conviction that his beloved mother and father not only are still around on some level, but are also letting him know that on a regular basis through signs and deeds that only he can identify.

Of course, these personal experiences alone are not proof of the existence of life after death or anything else, but for the authors it was enough to go on and begin the healing process.

Sometimes enough circumstantial evidence finally changes your mind and reconciles your beliefs with your experiences. That personal experience is what changes you, not the scientific journal articles and reports from clinical lab experiments that prove fact from fiction. When it happens to you, you know.

The Grid is real. And not only is it real, but we are an intrinsic and important part of it.

Much of the suffering we experience as humans comes from a feeling of separation from the bigger picture—oftentimes even from ourselves. War, murder, rape, abuse, poverty, torture, neglect . . . these actions and behaviors would be mostly eradicated if we understood that everyone is connected at this deeper, implicate level, and that we never end, and therefore death is not something to fear but rather celebrate as another part of the continuum. Who would care who was a liberal or a conservative, Jew or Christian if we knew that we were on a deeper level the same person, made of the same stuff? Why would we waste time fighting and railing against other people, even our environment, if we truly realized that we were a part of everyone, and everything?

How much more peace would we feel in our hearts if we knew that no one ever perished and that life went on, albeit somewhere other than our level of reality, and that our loved ones who have passed on would be there waiting? How much more happiness could we achieve if we slowed down the frantic grab for more, more, more, knowing that this life is just one among many that we get to experience? How much more love would we give if we knew other people couldn't really be taken from us?

Knowledge of the Grid could change not just how we see our world, but how we see ourselves. Reality, dear friends, would never be the same again. The Grid concept isn't by any measure the first or the last to suggest this, but we feel that giving a powerful visual context to the theory of connectivity and multileveled realities helps people to wrap their minds around something far too intimidating otherwise. Like infinity. Or love . . .

We know that we are immersed in these other realities. Too many signposts point to such a conclusion. Think of the microcosmic world of microbes and the teeming life that is visible only with the aid of a powerful microscope. Invisible to the naked eye, there is a reality that has its own rules and laws and order and we cannot see it until we specifically do something to perceive it, such as look through the lens of a scope. This applies as well to the macrocosmic reality of the universe beyond our visible eye, where black holes are churned out and fiery galaxies form and planets and stars are birthed. We see none of this, unless we look through the "eyes" of the Hubble Space Telescope or other such devices that allow us to see what we cannot unaided. And even our most amazing telescopes can barely glimpse into the farthest distances of the known universe, so we must then only imagine what lies beyond its confining boundaries.

What of other worlds? Other realities? Can we say they are not there because we cannot see them or prove their existence? Humans are not able to see many levels of the visual spectrum of light, such as X-rays or gamma rays, or hear levels of the audio spectrum, such as infrasound and ultrasound. We don't see what other creatures see, or hear what they hear, yet do we deem their experiences "unreal"? Because it is not a part of our daily routine, we shun it as being less than real to us, yet it is still real whether we like it or not.

Maybe it's an innate human arrogance that keeps us holding on to the sense of being special and separate from everything around us, even the unseen. If so, this arrogance certainly does not serve our best interests. It keeps us in fear. Fear of our own greatness, fear of others, even fear of death itself. Our level of the Grid has become our personal and collective comfort zone. But only when we get those glimpses of other realities are we able to grow and expand our vision of what is possible not only for us, but for humanity, for the planet and everything on it as well. Imagine knowing that we have access to worlds where we can speak to the "dead" or see creatures and life-forms that do not exist here on Earth, or possess the ability to know a person's thoughts and see things from great distances. Imagine knowing that nothing is permanent, but only in this level, and that people we love live on forever as they travel about the Grid.

Imagine realizing that our mundane existence means so much more than we thought it did, and that the world we have boxed ourselves into is actually much grander and more diverse than we could have ever imagined.

Better still, imagine that we are the Grid and the Grid is us, all of us combined, and we can access parts of it at will any time we want with a little knowledge, practice, and understanding of how these other levels intersect with ours, and what the triggers and mechanisms are that allow us to connect to them.

As stated in the introduction of this book, the Grid is a concept, an idea, a theory awaiting validation from our own continued research and that of countless others. We don't pretend to truly have valid proof of our version of reality, let alone the many other levels that likely exist. We don't have the mathematical ratios that will describe the physics behind it all, or the laboratory results of hundreds of experiments. But we do have the foundation of a collective body of ideas that affirms the one stunning conclusion that there is a hidden order to things. What we do believe is that we have presented an intriguing case of circumstantial evidence and valid ideas that provide food for thought. Actually, not just food, but a feast, ready to be consumed and digested.

The concepts that we have presented align with so many other concepts and theories, both metaphysical and scientific, and yes, even paranormal, that all seek to define and describe an infrastructure for what cannot yet be seen, yet is sensed and known and experienced by so many people throughout the ages. Our hope is to continue looking for the connectors, triggers, and mechanisms and discover how it all works together to create the Grid, and our role in its evolution. Each week, exciting new discoveries add to the discussion and dialog as more scientists look for the same connective web, whether those discoveries occur at the most cutting-edge particle physics labs or out in the field in nature. Every field of science has its share of clues to offer, its pieces of the puzzle of what reality is and how it might operate. From quantum physics to biology to neuroscience to geology, the world we live in is teeming with clues which all seem to point to similar conclusions.

Religion, spirituality, metaphysics, and the new emerging science of noetics are also seeking to define this until-now indescribable fundamental truth that reality is not a singular thing and that it actually has a form, albeit a hidden one, and a method to its madness. That method is evident in the effects we experience all around us, even if we cannot yet see the cause. It's like gravity, as we said before. We feel the effects of gravity every moment of every day, but we can't see it or hold it in the palms of our hands. And yet, we know that it exists.

The infrastructure of reality is like gravity. It leaves *tons of clues* for us to piece together, but we have to open ourselves up to perceiving those clues and not brush them under the rug of "junk science" or "pseudo mysticism" simply because nobody can tape them up on a wall or duplicate them at will in a controlled, clinical setting.

Many people reading this book have seen the Grid, even experienced a few of its many levels. Well, maybe they haven't "seen" the Grid in the way we are used to seeing things. It's almost as if, when it comes to the Grid, we have to sense our way around it using modes of perception that go far beyond our eyes, ears, and other body parts. Even our brains are not enough. Something more points us to the evidence of these other realities, and something more experiences them and processes them as something incredibly important, yet utterly frustrating in their subjectivity. And if you ask anyone who has been out Gridwalking, they will tell you this. In fact, some even see an actual grid-like structure in their visions, dreams, and mind's eye! Several people reached out to us to inform us of their visions during the writing of this book, citing imagery of an actual three-dimensional grid they envisioned in a dream or altered state of consciousness.

This intricate, connected thing that keeps us all bound by hidden web strings, this amazing multidimensional field of all matter and form and ideas and information and possibility and potential, this entirety of structure seen and unseen, this holographic image of which we are each a complete yet separate piece, this massive skyscraper with its many floors and staircases and elevators, this thing we call the Grid, we believe it is real, and we are part of it, and we are walking it every day during our waking state, our sleep state, and all states in between. We are all the Grid, swimming like fish in an ocean so vast we cannot even sense the scope of its magnitude.

We all too often believe only what we can see. Maybe all it takes to see the Grid is a slight shift in perspective, that one day very soon might reveal the hard evidence needed to close this case once and for all and release us from the limiting belief that "this is all there is." Sometimes we have to believe it *first* in order to open up the part of us that can see it. We cannot put the cart before the horse.

Faith. It's a funny word, as it usually implies a religious connotation. But when it comes to the invisible order of existence, even the most brilliant scientists have had the faith to accept the possibility that the small piece of knowledge that we humans can lay claim to is in no way the extent of the knowledge itself.

Just because you are one piece of the puzzle does not mean that you know the vastness and expansiveness of the entire puzzle. Not until you find your place in the interlocking scheme of things will you, or any of us, truly understand what the bigger picture truly is.

Happy Gridwalking!

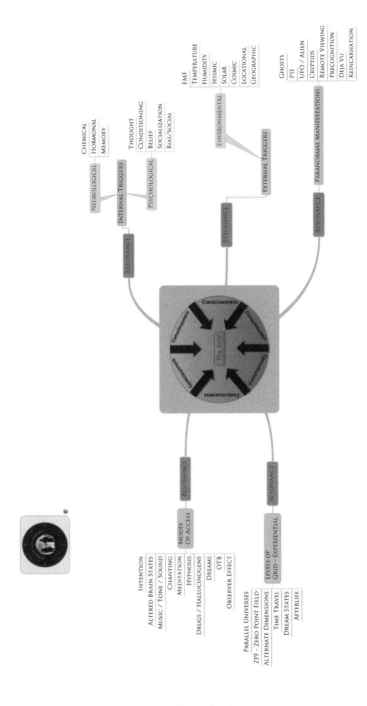

Figure 15. A version of the gridmap we used to look at the infrastructure, connectors, triggers, and mechanisms of the Grid. *Courtesy of Larry Flaxman and Marie D. Jones*

Acknowledgments

We would like to thank Lisa Hagan, agent extraordinaire, for all of her faith, hard work, and belief in us throughout the years. We would like to thank Randy Davila, Allison Jacob, and the entire staff at Hierophant Publishing for allowing us to write this book and believing in its message. We would also like to thank our families, friends, and readers for making this all possible and for putting up with our brutal writing schedules. It takes a village to write a book and get it out there, and we are so grateful for everyone involved!

Marie

I would like to thank my mom and number one cheerleader, Milly, for, well, *everything!!* Thank you to my wonderful sister Angella, who is my best friend, training partner, and fellow mischief-maker. I would also like to thank my brother, John, for all of his support and laughs, and my entire extended family. I'd also like to thank my dad, John, who is somewhere in the Grid looking down at me, smiling. He is responsible for my love of science and racehorses that continues to this day. In addition, my friends and colleagues mean the world to me, and they all know who they are, including my Wahines. Ron Patton, thank you for your support and cheerleading!

Thank you to all the people who took the time to read my books, contact me, and even friend me on social networks. Your support means everything, and without that kind of support a writer's work is meaningless.

Thank you to the team of people who are helping to make my dreams come true: Bruce Lucas, Helen Cooper, Italia Gandolfo, and Tammy Hunt. Thanks to the alumni of ProSeries 38 who have become my allies and friends in the writing adventure.

Thank you to the one and only Larry Flaxman, my partner and dear friend, for what seems like a lifetime of amazing interaction and achievement together despite it only being six years. Oh, the adventures we've had, the ideas we've dissected, and the conversations we've engaged in! And hopefully the adventure will continue with more projects down the road in the years to come. I cannot wait to see where we go!

Most of all, thank you to the center of my universe and the anchor in my life, my son, Max. He is my greatest passion and creation, and a really cool, amazing, and badass kid to boot! Max makes it all worthwhile—the good, the bad, and the ugly. His smile melts my heart, and when he calls me "Babs" the world is a good, good place.

Larry

First and foremost, I would like to thank my mom, Sheila, and my dad, Norman, for instilling all the traits that have made me the person I am today. Your passion and love for life have served as a template for me and have inspired me to be as impassioned in everything that I do. While you are no longer on this physical level of the Grid, I am certain that you are still with me, and I look forward to the day that we will be reunited. I love you both more than words.

I would also like to thank my wife Emily for putting up with my crazy working hours and travel schedule. You have always supported me in every endeavor and I am truly grateful.

I am thankful for all of my friends, fans, and associates who provide me with support, comments, advice, and affirmations that I regularly ask for (and sometimes even when I don't!). You guys and gals make it all worthwhile!

A special thanks goes out to William S. Harley and Arthur Davidson for founding the company that is ultimately responsible for building my personal escape pods from reality (a.k.a. the greatest motorcycles in the world). Your machines allow me to get away from the human level of the Grid and experience the closest thing to Gridwalking possible on Earth.

And Marie D. Jones, what can I say? I am so thankful that you are in my life. Looking back over the last six years I still fondly remember that very first email exchange when I praised your book *Psience*. Who would have known that we would become such good friends and crank out so many awesome books together? We truly are a force to be reckoned with. I look forward to the next six years and beyond—I have a feeling that the ParaExplorers will be unstoppable!

Finally, and most importantly, I want to thank my daughter Mary Essay (a.k.a. "the Honey"). Every single day you remind me of the inherent good in life. You are my ultimate masterpiece, and every time I look into your eyes I see the beautiful, incredibly intelligent person that you have become. Your sense of wonderment and inquisitive nature are so rewarding to see, and I am so proud to call you my daughter. I love you more than anything!

Bibliography

Barrett, Sir W. F. *Psychical Research*. London: Williams & Norgate, 1911.

Beauregard, Mario. *Brain Wars: The Scientific Battle over the Existence of the Mind and the Proof That Will Change the Way We Live Our Lives*. New York: HarperOne, 2012.

Bohm, David. *Wholeness and the Implicate Order*. London: Routledge, 1980. Reissued in 2002.

Brooks, Michael. "How Does Consciousness Fit In?" *New Scientist* 215, issue 2884 (September 29, 2012): 42–43.

Carrington, Hereward, and Nandor Fodor. *Haunted People: Story of the Poltergeist Down the Centuries*. New York: E. P. Dutton & Co., 1951.

Eliot, Alexander. *The Universal Myths: Heroes, Gods, Tricksters and Others*. Middlesex, England: Penguin Books, 1990.

Fodor, Nandor. *On the Trail of the Poltergeist*. New York: Citadel Press, 1958.

Ghose, Tia. "Weird Quantum Theory Works in Big Things." *LiveScience* (February 14, 2013). http://tinyurl.com/b3zg5lh.

Goldberg, Bruce. *Exploring the Fifth Dimension: Parallel Universes, Teleportation and Out-of-Body Travel*. Woodland Hills, CA: Bruce Goldberg, 2009.

Greene, Brian. *The Elegant Universe: Superstrings, Hidden Dimensions, and the Quest for the Ultimate Theory*. New York: Vintage Books, 2000.

———. *The Hidden Reality: Parallel Universes and the Deep Laws of the Cosmos*. New York: Vintage Books, 2011.

Hameroff, Stuart, and Roger Penrose. "Orchestrated Objective Reduction of Quantum Coherence in Brain Microtubules: The 'Orch OR' Model for Consciousness." In *Toward a Science of Consciousness: The First Tucson Discussions and Debates*, edited by Stuart R. Hameroff, Alfred W. Kaszniak, and Alwyn C. Scott. Cambridge, MA: MIT Press, 1996.

"The Heart Has Its Own 'Brain' and Consciousness." *Waking Times* (September 12, 2012). http://tinyurl.com/czcxlvn.

Hodgkinson, G. P., J. Langan-Fox, and E. Sadler-Smith. "Intuition: A Fundamental Bridging Construct in the Behavioural Sciences." *British Journal of Psychology* 99 (March 2008): 1–27.

Jones, Marie D. *PSIence: How New Discoveries in Quantum Physics and New Science May Explain the Existence of Paranormal Phenomena.* Franklin Lakes, NJ: New Page Books, 2007.

Jones, Marie D., and Larry Flaxman. *This Book Is from the Future: A Journey through Wormholes, Portals, Relativity and Other Adventures in Time Travel.* Pompton Plains, NJ: New Page Books, 2012.

Joseph, Channing. "U.S. Navy Program to Study How Troops Use Intuition." *The New York Times* At War blog (March 27, 2012). http://tinyurl.com/79e5xjk.

Jung, Carl G. *The Archetypes and the Collective Unconscious.* Collected Works, Princeton, NJ: Bollingen Series XX, 1959.

Kaku, Michio. *Parallel Worlds: A Journey through Creation, Higher Dimensions, and the Future of the Cosmos.* New York: Anchor Books, 2006.

———. *Physics of the Impossible: A Scientific Exploration into the World of Phasers, Force Fields, Teleportation and Time Travel.* New York: Doubleday Books, 2008.

Khajavikhan, M., A. Simic, M. Katz, J. H. Lee, B. Slutsky, A. Mizrahi, V. Lomakin, and Y. Fainman. "Thresholdless Nanoscale Coaxial Lasers." *Nature* 482 (February 9, 2012): 204–07. doi:10.1038/nature10840.

Krippner, Stanley, Adam J. Rock, Julie Beischel, Harris L. Friedman, and Cheryl L. Fracasso, eds. *Advances in Parapsychological Research 9.* Jefferson, NC: McFarland & Company Inc. Publishers, 2013.

Laszlo, Ervin. *The Akashic Experience: Science and the Cosmic Memory Field.* Rochester, VT: Inner Traditions Books, 2009.

Leggett, Hadley. "Out of LSD? Just 15 Minutes of Sensory Deprivation Triggers Hallucinations." *Wired* (October 21, 2009). http://www.wired.com/wiredscience/2009/10/hallucinations.

Lickerman, Alex. "The Problem with Reincarnation." *Psychology Today* (October 14, 2012). http://tinyurl.com/kwrzv6a.

McTaggart, Lynne. *The Field: The Quest for the Secret Force of the Universe.* New York: HarperCollins, 2002.

————. *The Intention Experiment: Using Your Thoughts to Change Your Life and the World*. New York: Atria Books, 2008.

Monroe, Robert. *Journeys Out of the Body*. New York: Broadway Books, 1992.

Moody, Raymond. *Life after Life*. Covington, VA: Mockingbird Books, 1975.

Myers, David G. "The Powers and Perils of Intuition." *Psychology Today*: 42–52 (November 1, 2002).

Pagels, Heinz R. *The Cosmic Code: Quantum Physics as the Language of Nature*. New York: Simon and Schuster, 1982.

Peake, Anthony. *The Labyrinth of Time: The Illusion of Past, Present and Future*. London: Arcturus Publishing, 2012.

Peat, F. David. *Synchronicity: The Bridge between Mind and Matter*. New York: Bantam Books, 1987.

Penrose, Roger. *Shadows of the Mind: A Search for the Missing Science of Consciousness*. New York: Oxford University Press, 1996.

Pfeiffer, Eric. "Heaven Is Real, Says Neurosurgeon Who Claims to Have Visited the Afterlife." Yahoo News (October 9, 2012). http://tinyurl.com/93vgcom.

————. "Whoa: Physicists Testing to See if Universe Is a Computer Simulation." Yahoo News (December 12, 2012). http://tinyurl.com/bbtkcbv.

Purdy, T. P., R. W. Peterson, and C. A. Regal. "Observation of Radiation Pressure Shot Noise on a Macroscopic Object." *Science* 339, no. 6121: 801–04 (February 15, 2013). doi: 10.1126/science.1231282.

Radford, Tim. "David Deutsch's Multiverse Carries Us beyond the Realm of Imagination." *The Guardian* (June 11, 2010). http://tinyurl.com/34m2oev.

Radin, Dean. *The Conscious Universe: The Scientific Truth of Psychic Phenomena*. New York: HarperOne, 1997.

————. *Entangled Minds: Extrasensory Experiences in a Quantum Reality*. New York: Paraview Books, 2006.

Randall, Lisa. *Warped Passages: Unraveling the Mysteries of the Universe's Hidden Dimensions*. New York: Harper Perennial, 2006.

Roll, William. *Unleashed: Of Poltergeists and Murder: The Curious Story of Tina Resch*. New York: Pocket Books, 2004.

Roney-Dougal, Serena. *Where Science and Magic Meet*. London: Element Books, 1991.

Rosenblum, Bruce, and Fred Kuttner. *Quantum Enigma: Physics Encounters Consciousness,* 2nd Edition. New York: Oxford University Press, 2011.

Russell, Walter. *A New Concept of the Universe.* Waynesboro, VA: The University of Science and Philosophy, 1989.

Segal, Nancy L. *Entwined Lives: Twins and What They Tell Us about Human Behavior.* New York: Plume, 2000.

Sheldrake, Rupert. *Morphic Resonance: The Nature of Formative Causation.* Rochester, VT: Park Street Press, 2009. Revised edition.

Stahura, Barbara. "The Ground of All That Is." *Science of Mind* (October 2012).

Stevenson, Ian. *Where Reincarnation and Biology Intersect.* Westport, CT: Praeger, 1997.

Strassman, Rick. *DMT: The Spirit Molecule.* Rochester, VT: Park Street Press, 2001.

Swanson, Claude. *The Synchronized Universe: New Science of the Paranormal.* Tuscon, AZ: Poseidia Press, 2006.

Talbot, Michael. *The Holographic Universe: The Revolutionary Theory of Reality.* New York: HarperPerennial, 2011.

Tegmark, Max. "Parallel Universes." *Scientific American* (April 14, 2003). http://www.scientificamerican.com/article.cfm?id=parallel-universes.

Tucker, Jim B. *Life before Life: Children's Memories of Previous Lives.* New York: St. Martin's Griffin, 2008.

Varghese, Roy Abraham. *There Is Life after Death: Compelling Reports from Those Who Have Glimpsed the After-Life.* Franklin Lakes, NJ: New Page Books, 2010.

Westerhoff, Jan. "Defining Reality." *New Scientist* 215, issue 2884 (September 29, 2012): 34.

Wiseman, Richard. "Common Brain Mechanisms Underlie Supernatural Perceptions." *Scientific American* (December 29, 2011).

About the Authors

Marie D. Jones

Marie D. Jones is the best-selling author of twelve books and writes the blog *Take My Life, Please . . . No Really, Take It!* She also coauthored with her father, geophysicist Dr. John Savino, *Supervolcano: The Catastrophic Event That Changed the Course of Human History.*

Marie has an extensive background in metaphysics, cutting-edge science, and the paranormal. She is a former licensed New Thought/metaphysics minister and has trained extensively in the Science of Mind/New Thought arena. In the 1980s and '90s Marie worked as a field investigator for MUFON (Mutual UFO Network) in Los Angeles and San Diego and she currently serves as a consultant and director of special projects for the Arkansas Paranormal and Anomalous Studies Team (ARPAST), where she works with ARPAST president Larry Flaxman to develop theories that can be tested in the field. Their current project, called the Grid, will be launched in 2013.

Marie has appeared on the History Channel's *Nostradamus Effect* and *Ancient Aliens*. She served as a special UFO/

abduction consultant for the 2009 Universal Pictures science fiction movie *The Fourth Kind.* as well as the science fiction film *Aurora.*

She has been interviewed on hundreds of radio programs, including *Coast to Coast AM* with George Noory, Whitley Strieber's *Dreamland* (which she also cohosts), *The Jeff Rense Show,* Jim Harold's *Paranormal Podcast, The "X" Zone* with Rob McConnell, the *Kevin Smith Show, Cut to the Chase, Feet to the Fire, World of the Unexplained,* and *Independent Expression (IE) Radio* with Shirley MacLaine.

Her essays and articles have appeared in *Whole Life Times, Light Connection, Vision, Conspiracy Journal,* and *Beyond Reality.*

Marie has lectured at major metaphysical, paranormal, new science, and self-empowerment events, including Through the Veil, Queen Mary Weekends, TAPS Academy Training, CPAK, Paradigm Symposium, Conscious Expo, and Darkness Radio Events.

LARRY FLAXMAN

Larry has been actively involved in paranormal research and hands-on field investigation for more than thirteen years. He melds his technical, scientific, and investigative backgrounds together for no-nonsense, scientifically objective explanations regarding a variety of anomalous phenomena.

He is the president and senior researcher of ARPAST, the Arkansas Paranormal and Anomalous Studies Team, which he founded in February 2007. Under his leadership, ARPAST has become one of the nation's largest and most active paranormal research organizations with more than 150 members worldwide. Widely respected for his expertise on the proper use of equipment and techniques for conducting a solid investigation, Larry also serves as technical advisor to several paranormal research groups throughout the country.

Larry has appeared on the Discovery Channel's *Ghost Lab* and the History Channel's *Ancient Aliens*. He has been interviewed for dozens of print and online publications, including *The Anomalist, The Times Herald, Jacksonville Patriot, Paraweb, Current Affairs Herald, Unexplained Paranormal Magazine,* the *Petit Jean Country Headlight,* the *Villager Online,* and *Pine Bluff Commercial.*

He has appeared on hundreds of radio programs all over the world, including *Coast to Coast AM* with George Noory, *TAPS Family Radio, Encounters Radio, Higher Dimensions* with Phyllis Pricer, *The "X" Zone* with Rob McConnell, *Ghostly Talk, EERIE X, Crossroads Paranormal Radio, Binnall of America, World of the Unexplained,* and *Haunted Voices Radio.*

Larry is a popular public speaker, lecturing widely at paranormal and metaphysical conferences and events all over the country, including major appearances at Through the Veil; History, Haunts, and Legends; Paradigm Symposium; ESP Weekend at the Crescent Hotel; The Texas GhostShow; and DragonCon.

Larry is also active in the development of cutting-edge, custom-designed equipment for use in the field investigating environmental effects and anomalies that may contribute to our understanding of the paranormal.

◎ ◎ ◎

Larry and Marie are both staff writers and official bloggers for *Intrepid Magazine* and their work has appeared in *TAPS ParaMagazine, New Dawn Magazine,* and *Phenomena.*

They cowrote the screenplay for the paranormal thriller *19 Hz,* which is in development with Bruce Lucas Films.

Both speak often at local and regional meet-ups, metaphysical centers, churches, libraries, and film festivals on the subjects of science, the paranormal, metaphysics, noetics, and human potential.

They currently cohost a radio show called *ParaFringe Radio* on the History FM/LiveParanormal Network.

In 2010 Marie and Larry launched their ParaExplorer series of e-books and articles, introducing readers to a variety of subjects, such as the science of the paranormal, life after death research, conspiracy theory, the time prompt phenomenon, and more.

Hierophant Publishing
8301 Broadway, Suite 219
San Antonio, TX 78209
888-800-4240

www.hierophantpublishing.com